Heart with Wings

by

Lisa Hitchcock

A Mother-Daughter Story
Inspired and Assisted
by
Nadia Hitchcock

RoseDog🐾Books

PITTSBURGH, PENNSYLVANIA 15222

ISBN: 978-1-4349-9511-7
Printed in the United States of America

First Printing

For more information or to order additional books, please contact:
RoseDog Books
701 Smithfield Street
Pittsburgh, Pennsylvania 15222
U.S.A.
1-800-834-1803
www.rosedogbookstore.com

I devote this writing to my daughter, Nadia.
My inspiration to continually persevere
And be the best I can be
and
To Mom and Dad
For always being in my corner
No matter what the odds.

Heart with Wings

This may read like fiction but it's not!

Introduction

Should I train to run a marathon or should I start my book? I proposed that very question to myself toward the end of last year. Life has been this roller coaster of highs and lows, but at least I've lived. Typically, when I hit the low points, I tended to pray harder to a higher power, my God. We all have a higher power helping us through the rough patches. I heard that voice, louder this time, insisting, "Be true to yourself, write your book!" I had a drawer full of material waiting to be assembled in some order. It is now, in retrospect, that I thank God for gently nudging me. I understand it was a process to help me heal and quiet my soul. A journey and tool to personally slay those demons and dust off the skeletons in my closet that felt more like a huge elephant in the room. Ditching the anger has helped free me to move toward an ultimate peace through this process. I highly recommend it! But you must also believe me when I say; I don't even pretend to have it all figured out. I am still waiting for more instructions each day. I am no longer feeling like a victim in my own life. Viva la fifty-something! I am trying to **control** less, worry less and enjoy the moment more. All of you women out there, 50 years and older, I hold you up in admiration for the awesome ladies you are and continue to make a difference in other peoples lives. If there is one key thing I have learned from this process, it is to fret less about tomorrow and focus on today. Tomorrow will become today soon enough and we must not let all that time in between go to waste. We have so much to contribute and to share. This life God gave us may not be the one we played out in our head but it is the best for us at the moment. He has given us what we need most to learn and grow and that is to be the best we can be.

Storm on the Horizon

I have never been much of a baseball fan but I suddenly find myself in a batting cage, of all places! The disturbing hum of a ball machine in the distance filling up with a new load of baseballs aimed right at me. The light blinks in the distance indicating a ball is about to fire in my direction and I am unprepared! Where are the bats? I search at my feet for something, anything to block the ball from hitting me. I'm all alone in here and to make things worse it is really dark—the middle of the night! I dodge the first ball but notice that light blinking again and another one follows shortly after. I feel the ball brush my hair almost hitting my left jaw. This familiar feeling of helplessness and desperation over my current dilemma causes my heart to race. The noise of the machine revs up as if someone deliberately kicked it into high gear. The balls accelerate the attack one after another. Thankfully my screams for help awaken me, at least for now. I look at the clock flashing 2:22 am. Again, like a re-run of the movie *Groundhog Day*, every morning this week, the same time, same dream. It may be just a dream but it symbolizes my life these days. That, no doubt, is why it keeps playing out in the form of a dream over and over. What is it that I have to learn from this before it goes away? I would really like to know.

My life has been in a state of limbo for the past couple of years now. I'm one of those *empty nesters* people refer to which describes parents who find themselves home alone once the kids go away to college. Some embrace the new lifestyle; others have a hard time with it. I am in the "hard time with it" camp. My house is particularly empty being that I'm single and alone for the first time in 18 years.

After my daughter's high school graduation, the two of us went on this glorious trip to Italy for two weeks. This would be our last mother-daughter trip before she moved to southern California to begin college. We had decided before this vacation we would get mother-daughter tattoos symbolizing our love and bond that could never be broken (a pretty big decision for a middle-aged woman if you ask me). We decided a **heart with wings** would be the perfect choice; a heart nestled in the middle of two wings. The heart symbolized our unwavering love and the wings represented Nadia's independence as she embarked on this new journey of her life.

We fell in love with this Italian paradise. How could you not? We stayed in Sorrento, a beautiful little *paese* with winding roads, crazy drivers and beautiful views of the Amalfi coast, and of course gorgeous Italian men. Everyone seemed to know just from looking at us that we were from California. They asked about it with such interest as if it were a country in itself. Who else would have a movie star for their governor? We enjoyed the Italian cuisine, especially the limoncello, an intoxicating lemon liqueur for which this region is known. It was the perfect vacation. The fact that I hadn't thought about work since I boarded that airplane in San Francisco was *un buon segno* (a good sign). I kept thinking the entire time I was there, "I could live in this place." It was apparent to me that these Italians really knew how to live life to the fullest. *La dolce vita* as they say, the sweet life.

We followed through with our tattoo plan. We chose to have our heart and wings placed on our lower backs just above the bikini line. I wanted to be more discrete with mine and choose when I wanted it to show. A heart with wings was truly the perfect choice.

Since all good things must eventually come to an end, we said good-bye to Italy but not until we had each thrown two coins over our left shoulder as tradition dictates while in Rome. The first coin was for love and the second to return to Italy some day. Neither one of us wanted to leave. I needed to get home and back to work to pay for the VISA bills we had run up while vacationing. Nadia was soon to embark on college life in southern California, a separation I had been anticipating and dreading for some time now. It was a new chapter unfolding for both of us.

During her first semester in college, Nadia wrote a heartwarming paper in her creative writing class about our tattoo experience and the symbolism behind it. It touched my heart to know that this moment meant as much to her as it did to me. She wrote:

"Indescribable, painful vibrations running down my back, the persistent buzzing of the needle soon becomes routine and blends with the voices that accompany. Feeling so virgin to this distinct sensation compared to the many bodies covered with color and designs surrounding me, I blankly stare at the eyes of sculls and dragons gawking at me from the pale, white walls. Is this really happening? Is he almost done? How does it look? So many questions pressing in my anxious mind. An audience gathers around to admire the artwork now permanently stained upon my back. I look for my mom's kind eyes for comfort and reassurance. Our love is the reason behind the ink.

A tattoo parlor is not normally chosen for a mother-daughter outing. After all, this is an unusual yet special occasion. Everyone has their own abundance of favorite things. I can tell you this, I am not a Harley-riding, leather-wearing, tobacco-spitting kind of girl. Just an innocent, shoe loving, smile wearing, sweetheart who now proudly wears a tattoo permanently placed on the low of her back. Some may wear a diamond ring or a pendant around their neck for the symbolism. Tattoos are talismans with the power to link us to the people we love and remind us of the things which are of utmost importance.

Anxious and prepared, I packed my whole life in suitcases and thought I was finally ready to move away from the simple life I had been engaged in for eighteen years. Although when it came down to it, my mom was the only thing I could not take with me. Even though I would have never admitted so at the time, I wasn't ready to completely let her go. How can we keep each other close while the miles separate us? This was the question which ultimately brought us to this tattoo shop.

An hour and forty-five minutes later, the artist said, "You are finished". Relieved, I stepped off the bench, trying to get my balance as my numbed feet finally touched the floor. I looked at my new reflection in the mirror. A beautiful heart with wings perfectly placed on my back. But it is more than just a tattoo; it's a symbol of love and independence. A mother-daughter bond that will never be broken and the strength to overcome all obstacles we may encounter, separately. The wings on my back will always be my mom, my angel lifting me up."

As her mom, I too proudly wear my heart and wings, a reminder of our love. Our tattoo symbolizes the many sacrifices and the unique path we've been on together for these precious twenty years as mother and daughter. No one can ever take that from us. With this incredible bond come stories, happy stories and some that we'd rather forget but we made this incredible journey together.

Mid-Life Crisis of Sorts

I've been so depressed since this stock market started its free fall at the end of 2008. I spent most of those last few months of the year coming home from work feeling mentally beat up. I'd get out of my work clothes and change into my favorite red abercrombie white moose head pj's. I sat at my computer, spending countless hours typing what ever came into my head. It was an unloading of all my pent up frustrations, some sort of needed release. Writing randomly seemed to help me make some sense out of my life dealing with my feelings of despair. Did I mention that I'm a stock broker? At home, I avoided the ringing telephone and considered my computer as my escape from the day-to-day drudgery of work. Each day at work meant endless, painful phone conversations with clients trying to offer them comfort and solutions to this crisis. It was difficult finding words to help at that time. Each situation was different but the goal was the same, trying to be optimistic while coming up with a plan to stop the effects of this market slide and at the same time being proactive and prudent. Bonds were getting hit. General Motors, Ford, GMAC, General Electric, Lehman, Morgan Stanley, Merrill Lynch, AIG. The list went on and on. Do we sell for fear of bankruptcy but lose three quarters of the principal as a result? Or do we do nothing and run the risk of losing it all in bankruptcy? Those were the scenarios we were trying to address, fifty-thousand dollar questions. Each day brought a new concern that another huge company was in financial trouble. It was one crisis after another lurking around the corner with no cut and dry answers. Many of my clients were retired and some widowed. They weren't prepared for this kind of shortfall in their portfolio values, nor were they in a position to earn the losses back in their lifetime. Where ever I went, people were talking about the stock market. At the grocery store, clerks were talking about their *401k* with customers, at the shoe store the radio was tuned to *market talk*, I couldn't escape it! As a result, a book was born.

I have kept journals throughout my life so this process of jotting down thoughts and ideas on paper from time to time isn't something new. But the plummeting stock market, a delayed reaction to corruption and greed, took the wind out of my sails and drove me into a seclusion of sorts. Writing about my feelings of loneliness, frustrations with my job and the difficulties that have come with this line of work seemed to help. Hours passed quickly while sitting at the computer typing as fast as I could to keep up with the thoughts that rushed into my head.

I had a drawer where I had been stuffing scraps of paper with scribbles and topics over the years, hoping to compile the material into a book someday. I finally emptied that drawer and moved the pile onto the floor next to my computer. I also stuck *Post-it Notes* along the edges of the screen as reminders of things I wanted to include. It felt good to finally put my words down in some order. It served a couple of purposes. First and most importantly, it took my mind off work and kept me occupied for hours at a time. This drawer was an accumulation of years of material needing to be written. That moment, when I first sat down to begin this process, I hit the *save as* icon on the computer and it asked, *save as what?* Good question, what should I name it? **Storm on the Horizon** became its first draft name. Random things initially, yet thought-provoking which is of course the purpose of writing. It took on a form of experiences and opinions on my current state of affairs. *A fifty-something woman just venting,* one might say, but you don't necessarily have to be a woman from my generation to understand my perspective and relate to the sadness brought on once your kids leave. How their absence magnifies a love-less marriage, or as in my case, divorced with no viable men in sight. It's easy to start feeling unnecessary, alone and undesirable. Men our age seem more interested in the twenty to thirty something women. What is the attraction when they could be dating women their own age who are more engaging, witty, wise and complex? Maybe dating younger women keeps men from having to face their own mortality.

I turned fifty four last October. I tried to blame my malaise on having another birthday. I have had work issues before. After all, I have been in the brokerage business twenty five long years so I have weathered my share of storms. But this one seems different. I'm more focused on the situation because this time I am completely alone, no distractions. Nadia is out of the house but still needs me financially and emotionally. We continue to protect those whom we hold dear, even when they don't live under our roof any more. It's the mother and her cub thing. Men in my life have continued to be disappointments so I'm faced with the idea that I may be alone the rest of my life. I'd like to be at peace with that fact if it plays out that way in the end. I'd like to share my future with a man, but not just any man. Someone who would enhance my life, not just fill a void. I've always taken care of myself, physically. Getting regular exercise and eating healthy, most of the time, has been an important part of my daily routine since college. I've recently added vitamins and supplements to my regimen but still feel out of sorts. Maybe it's hormones. At my age it's common to blame strange thoughts and abnormal behaviors on menopause but I don't think that is it, at least not at this time. Perhaps it is a delayed reaction to Nadia moving away. We talk by phone but it isn't the same. I am now living alone in this big house with my two cats. A scenario, I admittedly began worrying about when Nadia began her junior year of high school, already anticipating the pain and loneliness it would ultimately create for me.

I was in denial for the first six months she was gone. I made light of her being away when friends who knew our tight relationship asked how I was doing. "I'm fine", was my standard reply. "Her room is always clean and I now have time to take an Italian class at the local college. Maybe I'll go on one of those online match sites to find the man of my dreams. I'm ready now to find my prince charming. I have time to let a man in my life now that Nadia is gone." Looking back, I'm sure their concerns were validated. I felt so empty, a hole in the space where my heart used to be.

I call this quaint little town in northern California my home these days. Grass Valley, a part of Nevada County, put on the map during the California gold rush. Four years ago I moved from the country and bought this restored Victorian home built in 1898, within walking distance from town, restaurants and an old historic movie theater. It's a wonderful place to call home if you are a couple but it sucks for an attractive, working, single woman. Trust me!

By the way, I did try that *Dot.com* dating thing for a little while. I thought of it as a way to *extend my dating boundaries* by putting myself on one of these online dating sites. I had heard many success stories where people had met the person of their dreams. I wanted that! Well, I've now named that time as my *hitting rock bottom phase*. After setting up a profile and totally portraying myself truthfully, I discovered not everyone is as honest. Many of the men I encountered on these sites stretched the truth. They lied not only about their age, but past relationships and education (or lack thereof). They hid important facts which I would consider critical in the process of building a relationship based on trust. They seemed desperate to *reel me in like bait* and cement our relationship as one of *exclusivity*. I heard more than once from multiple prospects that at our age, it wasn't necessary to waste time dating for a long period of time. We should step it up a notch and choose the *fast-track dating* plan. *Fast-track?* Who would do that? I gave this *you've got mail* thing for six months (the length of my membership) and then turned the whole thing off. I prefer to find a partner the old fashioned way where you notice someone from across the room, lock eyes and your heart skips a beat. Empty words on paper and not so current pictures of men on a web site left me cold. One guy said in his profile, "I clean up real good". Maybe some woman would find that to be a turn on. Not this woman. I must admit though, it taught me a valuable lesson. I needed to stay out of my own way and stop trying to control my destiny.

It became evident by year end that the turmoil in the economy was not just a blip. Our world was in the middle of a financial meltdown. The worst financial crisis since the depression, maybe worse. No way of telling yet. I have weathered the ups and downs of market fluctuations over the years with clients, but this one seemed more difficult. I couldn't help picking up on the worry and concern in their voices and their tone was different. They needed someone to blame and I was the messenger that needed to be shot. Who wouldn't be worried? It impacted everyone. Even though history repeats itself, that fact was hardly a comfort. We lost confidence in everyone and everything.

This is a fickle business. Clients love you when things are going great, but when things don't go so well, they start to question your worth and want to know why you couldn't see this coming? Where was my crystal ball? Everyone is *risk tolerant* in a bull market but *risk adverse* when things go to *hell in a handbag*. Why couldn't I predict this? Would they feel more comfortable if our quarterly financial reviews included tarot cards and a palm reading? Needless to say, the circumstances were wearing on everyone and causing much trepidation and fear. Someone had to bare the brunt of the blame so I became their person. I was in the office daily at 5 am. I would wake up at 2:22 am unable to sleep from that recurring dream. I'd turn to the financial news channel to find the futures market (pre-market barometer) down another 100 points pointing to another volatile day in store. My heart spent a lot of time sinking to my stomach as it became evident that each day meant more pain and new problems. I was dodging bullets day and night. (Note to self: now I get it! That dream I keep having with the ball machine. It's a client turning up the speed!)

Product of My Environment

Humor me if you will, while I give you a little insight into my upbringing. No matter how hard we try, we are products of our environment and the apple doesn't fall far from the tree as the expression goes. We may desire to be different once we move from the house of our parents in search of our own autonomy and independence, however, the way we are raised and where we grow up has a huge impact on how we process decisions and conduct ourselves as grownups. Some of us embrace our childhood and use it as a tool to move forward, others stuff it, kicking and screaming, hoping to leave it in the past never wanting to visit there again. I look at mine like the carpet bag *Julie Andrews* carried in *Mary Poppins*. It's full of things that I have drawn from over the years that have given me strength to do battle. My bag contains skills and character traits I learned from my parents, such as tenacity, endurance, hope, independence, organization and control. Some I am happy I held on to, others not. I am terribly controlling and rigid. I worry too much. I am also a planner and a perfectionist. I'm working on the issues that border on being overly obsessive each and every day. Ideally our childhood is a process of baby steps and foundation building by our parents in preparation for adult life.

I was born and raised in Pasadena, California in the 50s. I was the first born and eldest of three girls born to Perry and Nancy in

1954. Pasadena is the home of the much revered *New Years Day Rose Parade* and *Rose Bowl Game*. When you live in Pasadena, everyone wants to visit you over New Years. It was also a part of my grandmother's dream that I would be chosen to be Rose Queen and ride on that prestigious float in the parade. OK, I admit, I did try out in this *quest for queen* for my grandmother in the 70s. But it was not to be. I made a couple of the cuts before coming up short. I came down with laryngitis the night before the semifinal elimination and couldn't talk during the interview phase. She said I would have won if I had not lost my voice. Bless her heart she was always my biggest fan. She had so much more confidence in me than I had in myself. I went into the process, knowing that I wasn't sophisticated enough, pretty enough, tall enough, or whatever it took to win, but it was a dream of many girls from Pasadena during that time....like a fairy tale. Now I realize having the mindset that I would not win was the very thing that most likely gave me laryngitis! Life works that way. Be careful what you set your intention on. Your mind is more powerful than you give it credit.

There was a lot more to Pasadena than just New Years festivities. It was a big city even then but had the feel of a small, close knit town where everyone knew each others business, so it seemed. I like to refer to it as being a Pasadenian like a religion (or disease). Webster doesn't recognize that term, but indulge me if you will. Being from Pasadena was like belonging to an association of sorts, with unwritten bylaws of *dos and don'ts*. I didn't realize while growing up that it would leave such a lasting impression and cause some consternation at different crossroads throughout my life. Our parent's beliefs and parenting styles during childhood don't just guide us when under their roof and then the slate gets wiped clean. They continually play key roles in the way we approach adulthood and parent our own kids even though we may make a conscious effort to be different.

It was a different generation back then. The men traditionally went to work while the women kept the home and took care of the children. All of my friends had two parents, a father and a mother. My mother, like most of the women in the community, belonged to ladies groups and followed the words of Ann Landers. My sisters and I were raised by two Bibles, the Word of God and Dr. Spock. In school, the girls were required to take home economics with classes in sewing, making perfect corners when making a bed, cooking and walking with proper posture. I was selected as Miss Posture Princess in junior high. I kid you not! We were brought up to go to college and ultimately get married and raise a family. Graduating from high school meant you were given a genuine pearl necklace (you could tell they were genuine when the pearl felt rough when you bit down on them with your teeth. If they were smooth, they were not the real deal). To be proper, the white shoes had to go into storage the day after Labor Day, not to be worn again until Easter. Don't ask me why, it was in a book of etiquette that everyone read I suppose. Random rules that were passed down from generation to generation and no one questioned the silliness of many. Whenever an invitation came in the mail for an upcoming wedding, my mother would turn it over and say, "See Lisa, you can tell this is a real engraved invitation". I studied it trying to understand the significance. You could feel the words through the back of the invitation like Braille. This was how a classy invitation was supposed to look according to my mother, right down to the enclosure card and stamped envelope to reply.

All that trivia aside, Pasadena was actually a great place to grow up. Kids in the neighborhood playing softball outside, their parents socializing at block parties and open houses during the holidays. The *Helms* bakery truck predictably drove down our street every afternoon and I'd run out with quarter in hand to get my favorite treat, a cream puff. We would think nothing of imposing on a neighbor to borrow a cup of sugar rather than making an extra trip to the store. It's what neighbors did back then. There were long games of kick the can and hide and seek with the neighborhood kids. Once the street lights turned on, it was our signal to go in for the evening. We all ate dinner every night together and we were not allowed to answer the phone during that time. If it rang my dad would say, "Who would be calling at this time, don't they know it's the dinner hour?" Did everyone eat at the same time back then? No evening soccer games or quick bites at *McDonalds* to interrupt the routine. It was dinner every night, together without fail.

Mom insisted we be fully dressed to go into town, no cutoff shorts, bathing suit tops or lounging attire allowed in public. Those were very prim and proper times. One oddity to me was the frequency at which women would go out in public in those pink squishy curlers while their husbands were at work. They would wear hair nets or scarves over these rollers which didn't really do much to hide them at all. Personally, I wouldn't have been caught dead in those things. I was always so self-conscious about how I looked in those days. I would never even go outside the house in my head gear when I had braces. Wow, have things ever changed! Some of the outfits people wear out in public these days are shameful. I'd fit in just fine at *Starbucks* in my red moose pj's but my upbringing won't allow it.

When I was growing up kids were expected to learn to play a musical instrument. While my friends got to choose fun things like the guitar or drums, my sisters and I had the *choice* taken out of the equation. We were going to play the piano. Our teacher was this rather large, spinster woman who lived with her mother and many cats. She barged into our house every Tuesday and Thursday morning, before school, to give us our piano lessons. It seemed like torture at the time. What kid looks forward to awakening at 6:30 in the morning to play Bach, Chopin and Beethoven to the clang of the metronome before school while the rest of the neighborhood slept? As if that wasn't enough, our parents insisted we join a group of musicians called Tuesday Musical Juniors. It met on Saturday morning! Go figure? That meant one precious Saturday a month was ruined - a day that was supposed to be reserved for play. Here we sat at the musical, in a library, listening to other kids and adolescents playing an array of musical instruments for a couple of long, boring hours. We wised up over time, filled our purses with food and ate in the bathroom lamenting our fate.

Sure, we complained and wished we could be more like other kids but looking back I feel fortunate I was raised in this suburban neighborhood by very loving, devoted parents. My sisters and I were raised to be responsible, God fearing adults. My parental influence continues to impact my decisions to this day and in the way I have parented my daughter for the most part. They stressed the importance of education, showing respect to others, honesty and speaking the English language correctly. You *lay* an object on the table but a person *lies* down; cakes and pies are *done* but people are *finished*. In our household, bad grammar was not tolerated! We didn't argue much as kids and we did as we were told up until the teenage years. Dad claims to this day that having three teenage girls in the house at one time caused him to go grey and lose most of his hair. Looking back, I'm sure there was a great deal of accuracy in that statement.

I don't resent the foundation my parents mapped out for me. I felt safe, and loved growing up, trusting that my parents knew what was best for us. Maybe so much that I was looking at life through rose colored glasses. Once I was out on my own, I found that the real world, at times, wasn't very nice. While growing up in my parent's home we were expected to be accountable for our chores and obligations. The house ran very efficiently most of the time, because we each carried our weight and could count on one another. I grew up having trouble giving myself permission to be happy until all my chores were finished and all my obligations fulfilled. That has continued to plague me in my adult life. I still catch myself trying to get every duck in a row and every chore accomplished before I allow myself to go out and have fun. It is as if I keep putting off happiness. Being aware of the problem is the first start to recovery they say! I'm working on this and probably will be until the day I die. It's a part of my DNA I'm afraid. My parents were also very private people and therefore taught us to keep our problems to ourselves within the family nucleus. On the one hand I was fortunate to have my family to lean on whenever I felt my world crashing in, however, as a result I've had a hard time opening up and admitting when I needed help in relationships out side the family and found it difficult to trust others.

I played by the rules growing up. Most of the kids I knew did. We respected our parents and spoke to other adults only when we were spoken to. Now it seems like all I do is constantly fight rules and the status quo. When I became an adult, I didn't fold perfect bed corners or sew much more than a Halloween costume. I didn't become a women's club groupie or join a bridge club. In fact a room full of women can really get on my nerves after a period of time. I didn't inherit the *gift of gab*. Unfortunately, it is easier for me to carry on a conversation with men. I'm better versed in stock market jargon or the latest sporting event than exchanging recipes or book club recommendations.

I was born an overachiever and always sought perfection in every-thing I took on. Maybe it's that *first born* syndrome. I've always been a control freak, a right brain thinker, a stickler to detail, overly organized and a compulsive worry wart. That's pretty much me in a nut shell. I assumed my obligatory position in the family pecking order early on as first born and tried to obey my mother's wishes to set a good example for my sisters. That was way more pressure than I signed up for. I have gone through life trying to be perfect and set good examples, being the best that everyone else wanted me to be. It has been exhausting, and near impossible in my line of work. I set myself up for failure more than reward.

Means to an End

I started writing when I was young, writing plays for the neighborhood and letters to people I admired. I wrote my innermost thoughts in a diary which I kept hidden so no one would know my true heart. I didn't want to share my secrets with anyone, my insecurities, my inadequacies that were a part of me as a child and then trickled over into adolescence and then adulthood. I've continued writing even when I wasn't physically putting words to paper; writing instead in my mind and comparing experiences as a way to get distance from things unpleasant. I tried to find patterns in relationships that had gone badly hoping to break the patterns that ultimately led to the painful breakup. Easier said than done I'm afraid. I did my share of *stuffing* and admit being *in denial* and *at fault* in too many situations to count. Every once in a while I would go into that closet and visit my skeletons.

It's All in a Name

I name things that I care about, I always have. Not just a daughter or a pet, but cars, houses, occasions, you name it...I name it! It's a way of saying to this person, place or thing "All right now, you are important to me so take care of us". The goats were named before they came into our lives to assure their safe arrival. I figure that once they have a name, they truly belong and become an important part of the family. Our white Jeep Cherokee was *Merry Legs*, the Dodge truck, *Delilah*. Our Ford F150 had to have a strong name for the tasks at hand, therefore she was *White Fang*. (They are all female by the way, surprised?) Then the silver Nissan Pathfinder with iron bumper guards was given an Italian name, *Isabella* as a conscious effort on my part to suppress my *rigid* German heritage and become Italian by choice. When it was Isabella's turn to drive to southern California to protect Nadia at school, I bought *Bella Nero* (Black Beauty) who I drive to this day. We named our Pike house *The Money Pit* for obvious reasons and my house where I reside now in Grass Valley is *Freedom*. Maybe I should have pre-named my men to assure better results. Such as *Knight in Shinning Armor* or *Daddy Warbucks...Romeo* perhaps?

Back to my storm brewing on the horizon speech. It has felt, lately, like I am on the brink of some big changes. It is an unsettling feeling that I can not quite put my finger on. Nadia often says, "Mom, don't worry, you just don't do change well". But that isn't necessarily true. I've weathered many changes in my lifetime and I'm ready to hit new ones head on. I'd just like to know ahead of time what they are. It's that need to control part of me. Is it going to take the form of a giant tsunami off shore or will it be a good change? We never really know. Is this huge drop in the stock market supposed to be a sign that I've done this long enough? Could I start something new, a new career at fifty four years old? I'm not embracing such an idea at this juncture but then again we're not always in control of our own destiny. My major in school was Psychology. If I pursued a career in that field, I'd need more schooling. Who's going to bankroll that endeavor? It's hard enough paying my mortgage and Nadia's college and living expenses in this ailing economy we find ourselves in.

It's uncanny how my life seems to mirror the trends of middle-America. After all, I'm a part of the baby boomer generation. An association I'm embarrassed to be a part of at this stage of my life. I believe it has ruined so many traditions such as marriage, relationships between men and women and even corporate America as we know it. We seem to have lost our edge as a country. We, as baby boomers really started the trend of jumping from job to job looking for the best deal rather than staying put. We also found ourselves in a world where companies began outsourcing and thinking nothing wrong with firing employees by e-mail. Baby boomers wanted to be forward thinkers, the *have everything now* mentality. What happened to the days when you stayed at the same job throughout your life and could look forward to a pension for life and health plan? What happened to marrying your childhood sweetheart, raising children as a couple and leading content and productive lives? We were born stirring the pot, compelled to change the status quo, *color outside the lines*, *hit the bricks running*, whatever you want to call it.

My parents never bought anything on credit. They waited until they could afford it and yet, I never remember doing without as a child. Now every week I get mail from some credit card company offering my daughter an American Express card or VISA.

Who do they think are going to be responsible for that bill she runs up? They don't really care. She has no track record of ever paying anything off herself. I probably could get the cats their own VISA cards without much effort.

The Viet Nam war didn't help things back in the 60s. It seemed to divide the youth and their parents. Very much the situation we have created today in IRAQ. Then there was the Beatles movement, women *burning bras at Woodstock* and a new generation of women making mockery of the role of the housewife. We were the pot-smoking generation and watched the rise in divorce rates and trends away from family values. It was a shift in focus to careers and fast cars. As a woman living during those times, I remember a shift in priorities. We wanted to be heard and compete with men for their high paying corporate jobs. Equal work and equal pay. What does that mean anyway? Has it really worked for most of us? Now women are working and managing their households; often working multiple jobs and raising the kids. There's a disturbing trend toward babies born out of wedlock or with no fathers at all. The family nucleus has broken down and the roles of men versus women are no longer defined. This isn't what I want for my daughter.

Faded Dreams

By the time I graduated from college, I wanted so badly for people to take me seriously, to be understood and to have a career where I felt needed and respected. I enjoyed college and sorority life as a Kappa Alpha Theta but it didn't represent reality for me. I wanted to get out in the real world and make something of myself. But even after all that schooling, I felt unprepared. I settled into clerical positions because I wasn't able to get a job with a bachelor's degree in my field of study. I lost touch with college friends and moved to the Newport Beach area. I spent much of my 20s trying to please everyone all the time and continued to flounder. Who was I? Who did I want to be?

I decided to take a job working at the mental health unit of a hospital in Santa Ana. At least I would be working toward a job more in line with my major in school. That was a painful dose of reality. I basically *babysat* delusional, suicidal, and anorexic patients in such pain mentally that they were subjected to a 72 hour hold, due to an episode that deemed them unable to be out in society. That job was the catalyst for deciding this field wasn't for me.

I made another mistake around that time. I married a German citizen whom I had been dating for the last three years. The marriage lasted less than two years, but at least we didn't have children. He was quite the womanizer and saw me as his opportunity for U.S. citizenship. My parents supported me in this wedding even though they had their doubts. The night before we were to get married my intuition told me it was wrong. I went out for a run and cried. I wanted to do the right thing, which would have meant putting a note on the church door explaining that the wedding was cancelled. I was too ashamed at that point and concerned about what people might think?

Me, a Stockbroker?

Would I really be able to do that? I was working as an executive secretary for a publicly traded medical products company when I became interested in the whole Wall Street thing. The company I was working for went public while I was working there and I was involved in the process of obtaining FDA approval, typing and submitting reams of paperwork, tombstones, and prospectuses. As employees, each of us had the opportunity to buy restricted shares of stock. It was fascinating. One of the girls I was working with said, "You would be good at that". "Good at what?" I remember asking. She said "working as a stock broker. They are hiring women now, they train you and you have the potential to make good money." The more I thought about the idea the more I liked it. I put a resume together and knocked on doors of major firms in the Orange County area. This was the early 80s and it was still very much a male dominated business. The brokerage firms hired up to thirty trainees into their programs annually and among those hired, a few were women. Smith Barney offered me a spot in their upcoming class beginning January 2, 1984. I was so excited. A new year and a new career! I showed up that first day dressed in a business suit and was given a huge box of study material. My job over the next sixty days was to learn all the material and take the day-long Series 7 Exam on St. Patrick's Day. If I passed, I'd be on my way to a month of training in New York. If I didn't pass I was out of a job. The regional manager, responsible for hiring me, said he hired me because of my tenacity and drive. I think it was because we both were USC grads! Whatever the reason, it didn't matter at that point, I got the job and I wasn't going to let them down. I was determined to be the best!

I met my parents for lunch and shared the good news. My dad was less than enthusiastic. He had years of experience in the securities business on the institutional side, different from retail, but still had concerns that it wouldn't be a good fit for me. Some of the descriptive adjectives he used with reference to the business included *cut throat, dog eat dog* and *ruthless*. What he didn't realize was I had already made up my mind. I wanted to make him proud. I was the first born and had always wanted to please him since a very young girl. Here was my chance to prove all the skeptics wrong. In retrospect I wish I hadn't been such a *know-it-all* and had taken his advice. It would have saved me so much grief and heart ache. I thought I knew so much back then and really knew nothing much at all. It's recommended that we spend a portion of our day, every day, listening to the words of the elderly and to children. If we did we would gain such wisdom. Advice I should have paid attention to back then. I realize now that my dad was just trying to help protect me from ultimate pain but I interpreted his lack of support as a sign he didn't believe I could succeed at this. What he forgot was he raised a head-strong daughter who was resilient and a fighter. I studied day and night for those next few months and passed that broker exam. I went on to become #1 in my training class and on my way to a career that I was proud of, so it seemed.

Keep Your Chin Up

I chose this career in true *boomer* fashion, officially bucking the trend of my mother and that of her mother, to be my own person. Was it out of rebellion or just wanting to be noticed or heard? An effort to join the fight against the establishment and buck the trend of past generations? I believe it was a combination of all the above. Wanting something different from ordinary and choosing a career over homemaker.

The USC degree in Psychology was chosen because it was interesting not sensible, especially if I wasn't going for a Masters or PhD. I didn't think past the here and now. Smart girls would major in education, nursing or music so they could *have something to fall back on* when they got married and raised their families. That was not going to be my life, no sureeee! I was going to carve out my niche among those *good old boys* and show them I was just as capable at doing their job, even better. I can now say, looking back in hindsight, that it has been a huge mistake. Not that I didn't do their job better because I did and still do. I've made a decent living which afforded me a great deal of flexibility while raising a daughter, but I've suffered the repercussions of working along side some pretty unethical sorts lacking basic moral values. I have made a living putting client's needs first unlike many of my male counterparts. I have always been a broker with a conscience and desire to always do the right thing. I honestly believe that what we do in life echoes in our eternity.

While working at Smith Barney I met a broker who had been in the business for about 10 years and we became friends. We had what seemed to be a great deal in common and we ultimately got married. We had our ups and downs but thanks to that union I gave birth to my only child, Nadia, my true joy in life. Her father was responsible for introducing us to Nevada County when we attended a wedding of one of his friends shortly after our marriage in 1987. Little did I know at the time that Nadia and I would ultimately call this area home?

Life in Pike

My favorite time, my happiest time was my life in Pike. I went out on a limb when Nadia's father and I parted ways. I didn't want to stay in southern California another minute. Ever since that wedding in the Nevada City and Grass Valley area I longed to go back and spend more time there. It was beckoning me to return. So I packed the car with the basic necessities and moved Nadia and me to the country. The move to northern California was initially an escape from city life and a doomed marriage. It had become evident things weren't working out with Nadia's father. His three children from his previous marriage ranging in age from 6-12 had unexpectedly come to live with us. We were all miserable, victims of circumstance thrown together abruptly without choice or preparation. I packed the car and left southern California. I headed north with Nadia and our cat Misha. I was petrified of the unknown ahead of me but sure I needed to leave my current situation. I had no idea this journey would impact our lives in such a positive way. I continued work as a stock broker, having to basically start over again gathering clients and assets. I tried to teach Nadia the important lessons in life by example rather than filling her with words of wisdom since I didn't feel very wise. Close to 40 years old and soon to be divorced. I was in search, once again for something to bring purpose to my life. This time, I had more than just myself to be responsible for. I missed my family but wanted to do what was in the best interest of Nadia, no matter what the stakes. I reflected often on that first day in the hospital when Nadia was born. Twenty eight hours of labor, 2 epidurals and a "C" section later she arrived. The long, anticipated union with my daughter, that precious little bundle with those beautiful blue eyes locking mine in ultimate trust. Together for the first time, a mere hour old, I made her a promise. I would give her my all, my 110%, no less. I finally understood my purpose in this life, to be her mom. I didn't want any regrets, this was far too important.

Looking back, now that she is all grown up, I can say that being her mom over the past twenty years has been the only real thing that has mattered. That unconditional love where you'd stop a speeding train to save her, take a bullet for her, do anything to keep her from being hurt. She's now away at school and probably out of the house for good, yet I will always be her mom, still parenting, counseling and holding her hand from a distance. Thank you *Verizon*! I just want her safe and sheltered from the pain I've endured trying to find love and be loved. I want her to find a special guy who will respect her, cherish her yet not try to squelch her independence. Is that too much to ask? Are there young men out there like that who are worthy of her love? I am afraid that my need for independence kept me from some quality relationships over the years. Hopefully, Nadia will find a balance between the independence and desire for companionship. I built this wall over the years to protect my heart from the creeps in my business and the men who seemed intrigued and curious by my strength and independence.

When we first moved to Nevada County, I rented a little house in Nevada City for a few years. I stumbled, quite by accident, on this home for sale in a little town in Sierra County by the name of Pike. It had a volunteer fire department and a little country school; that was it! It was a forty minute drive along a steep and winding two lane road from town. I called the real estate broker and offered quite a bit less than the asking price. I was actually shocked when my offer was accepted! Like it or not, I was suddenly a homeowner. I had a house, twenty acres of pine trees, two ponds and an ATV. I'll never forget when I first showed it to Nadia. She said, "But I really wanted a house with a yard mom!" What a funny comment, I thought at the time. To me, it had more yard than I knew what to do with but then I realized *yard* to her meant a fenced-in area with a dog inside. We ultimately made that happen.

At the time I had no idea how this house, this life and a relation- ship with a man would touch my heart and change my life for the better over these next eight years. The house and the country life quieted my heart and allowed me to be myself, the *self* I had been searching for my whole life. I fell in love with a man who lived up there. He had an admirable strength of character, a ded- ication to his passions and loved my daughter. Over the years we enjoyed many happy hours together making great meals, playing games, helping Nadia with her homework assignments and just enjoying each other. This was so new for me. I could be myself and he loved me anyway. This connection with him not just for the physical pleasure but it was the ultimate companionship.

I had a lot to learn about country life but I was eager and filled with anticipation at the idea of owning my first home. It was all mine and I couldn't wait to get started on my first project....my garden. I chose the location and began digging the holes for the posts and secured each one in cement. I weeded the area and en- closed it with seven foot fencing to keep the deer out. At the first hint of spring I planted everything I love: basil, lettuce, chard, asparagus, corn, butternut squash, sage, thyme, rosemary and lavender. Then to my surprise, it started snowing again around Easter. I thought it was spring? I panicked for fear of losing every- thing. I covered the ground and all my little seedlings with tarps, hoping they'd survive and not die of frost. That year was the best crop I ever had because it was in the ground too early I didn't know any better!

I had always dreamed of living in a home with a big, beautiful, green lawn. This house was set back from the front with a circle drive encompassing a yard about the size of half a football field.

I could have my beautiful lawn with a little work. I pictured us in white outfits playing croquet and sipping mint juleps enjoying the summer evenings. I know what you must be thinking…what a hopeless romantic! It's true; I love to dream big! After work I made numerous trips to a place in town called *Rare Earth*. They sold rock and soil by the truck load. You could drive your truck up to the loaders and they would drop your order into the back of your truck bed. Just as easy as the drive up window at *McDonalds*. I learned after the first trip it was important to water this top soil before exiting or you lost much of the load out the back while driving home. It must have attracted some attention when I'd stop at the hose before leaving the place, still in my business suit and heels watering down the pile of soil in the back of my truck. I had no choice but to still be in work clothes since home was twenty-seven miles due north. Once at home and changed into old clothes, I drove the truck onto the area designated for lawn some day and proceeded to shovel the top soil out by hand over the seed I had spread. Well, at this rate it was going to take me two summers to get this done. I decided to call *Rare Earth* and ask if they delivered. "They said yes, where do you live?" When I replied, Pike, they said, "It will cost you more to come that distance!" Of course it will! I learned that was the standard reply whenever I needed anything done up there. "It'll cost you more to come to Pike". It got tiring and expensive after a while. But this time it is was worth every penny.

Nadia and I pulled into the driveway that afternoon after the delivery and there was this beautiful pile of manure, a sight for sore eyes. The pile of stinky top soil was as tall as the roof of the pump house. I was so excited to get started. I changed into my grubby clothes and started spreading this stuff on top of my grass seed. Well, the stench attracted pesky little gnats that loved to fly around your eyes and become a real nuisance. I was not going to let these pests ruin my project but wasn't getting anywhere shooing with one hand and trying to finagle the shovel with the other. I rummaged through the garage and found an over-the-head net a neighbor gave me to keep the mosquitos away. It would be perfect as long as the gnats couldn't fly through the opening at my shoulders. I opened the trunk of Nadia's dress up stuff and found a pink sash to tie around my neck. "Perfect, they can't get me now", I said to myself and marched back out to continue my spreading. Unaware of the passage of time, Nadia startled me when she came out to inquire about the timing of dinner. She took one look at me and doubled over in hysteria. I must have looked ridiculous but that was the beauty of living there. No one ever dropped in or drove by except the few neighbors around our road. They all had similar wardrobes so we thought nothing of it. I had a favorite green and brown fleece jacket that mom and dad gave me from *L.L. Bean* my first Christmas in Pike. It hung conveniently by the front door. It was what I put on before going out in the yard day or night, winter or summer. I wore it while stoking the burn pile and the embers, which over time, left little holes in the back. We kept shoes by the front door that were easy to slip on and off. We learned that it was a good idea to pound the heel down on the deck before putting the shoes on. Stink bugs and spiders would make the toes *home* over night. Nadia put a foot in her boot before checking once and let out a scream that made my heart stop. She never liked any bugs, especially in her shoes. (The spiders loved her shower so it became routine for me to remove them each morning before she would get ready for school.)

Sorry, I've become sidetracked again, back to the lawn story. It was well worth the effort I'll have you know. By the fall it was lush and green. It took half a day to mow. I didn't invest in one of those fancy ride mowers. No, not this little worker bee. I did it the hard way. I had a gas mower with one of those levers that helped it move forward without a lot of effort as long as the ground was level, which it wasn't. The first start of the year was always hard. It would take numerous times pulling that cord upward (sometimes in excess of 10 or 15 times) before it would stay running. My arm and shoulder were sore for days after that first mow. The rest of the year it would start right up provided I kept gas and oil in it. One time I messed up and put gas where the oil went and oil where the gas was supposed to go. I didn't notice the little diagram showing me which was which. I had to take the mower to a *small machine repair* guy in town and have him flush it out. I put arrows and wrote with a black sharpie pen where gas went so I didn't make that costly mistake again. Nadia did the same thing for me inside on the computer with our passwords and important instructions. She had a little notebook for me labeled *instructions for dummies* (that's for you mom!) next to the computer. Bless her little heart.

Over the years I began to question my sanity over this lawn business. The maintenance and upkeep for a perfectionist like me was cumbersome to say the least. It wasn't just the mowing, but the patching and filling in to keep it looking great. Then the moles and/or gophers moved in (I'm not sure how to tell the difference). These varmints dug tunnels everywhere. I'd go outside in the morning and find little piles of fresh dirt all over; proof they had been busy all night long! I tried all the remedies; *Wrigley's* gum down in the holes, little dynamite-looking sulfur sticks that had to be lit by a match and shoved down the hole to snuff them out and finally resorted to a garden hose running water through the tunnels to drown them out. I ran the hose for what seemed liked hours. No water ever came up. It was hopeless. I gave up that battle, admitted defeat and resorted to flattening the piles every morning, sprinkling a little grass seed over the top and calling it good.

We had two really hot summers followed by very little rain and snow which left the forests extremely dry. I'd make a dump run every Saturday morning 10 miles up the road. Nadia often slept in until noon so I left her at home. On one occasion, coming back from the dump, I drove in and saw this unfamiliar truck idling in our driveway with two wolf-husky mix dogs in the back barking their heads off. I jumped out of my truck and ran to the door to find out what this pervert was doing trespassing on my property and talking to my daughter at the front door. He didn't look like he had bathed or shaved for over a week and when he introduced himself his teeth were yellowish brown. By now our Labrador retriever was barking because his dogs wouldn't shut up. He said, "I'm your neighbor on the back end of your property and you have beetles in your trees. They will eventually eat your entire forest if you don't do something and then they'll spread to mine." He gave me the creeps. I thanked him as graciously as I could for letting me know and said I'd take care of it. He just stood there so I grabbed Nadia and we both went in the house and locked the door. I called the logger who lived in town and asked him to take the trees down that were infected with these beetles. He explained that these pests attack trees that are in a weakened state as a result of the drought. Great! Now I had weak trees, what next? After that ordeal I had gates installed at each driveway to discourage future trespassers.

That same hot summer was a scary one for the whole town. There was an arsonist on the loose in Pike. Every week there was a new little fire, deliberately started but luckily put out in time by our volunteer fire crew before spreading and causing real damage. It was frightfully unsettling to drive to work each morning hoping whoever was doing this didn't succeed in burning down the entire town. I worried about the animals and kept cat carriers by the front door during that time so we could make a quick get away if necessary. It was extremely dry everywhere and if a fire wasn't put out right away it would have raged out of control in no time. There were only two ways to get out of Pike and one was way too steep and narrow to consider unless it was an emergency. It was appropriately named *Hells Half Acre*.

The volunteer fire crews were baffled. Why would anyone do such a thing? Then one night while everyone was sleeping a fire was set next to the bedroom window of the fire chief's house and burned up the side of their house before it was put out. No one was hurt but they wondered why the dog had allowed someone so close to the house to be able to set the fire. That's when the arsonist confessed. It was the fire chief's wife. She was trying to get his attention and unfortunately felt that setting fires was the only way to be heard. Well, she got attention alright in the local jail where she was ultimately sentenced to psychiatric evaluation.

While living in Pike, my mind quieted. I was physically active, always outdoors doing something and I could feel the stress of the work week melt away when I was on my property puttering. I frequently took walks all the way to the back of my property, talking to God, thanking Him for all this beauty around me. I never took it for granted. At night I would look forward to a glass of wine out on the porch swing admiring the full moon which would light up the sky. I loved listening to the frogs making happy croaking noises from my pond. When the moon wasn't full the stars were so vibrant they looked close enough to touch. If you watched long enough you could always catch a falling star or two. On the evenings when our friend came to dinner we'd get out the Monopoly game or lag coins against the front door. He loved to teach Nadia new dice games. They would shake the dice in cups and throw them out on the counter while I created some delicious feast for dinner. He loved to help her with her math homework and find some way to make it fun.

Those were my happiest days, the Pike days. I felt more joy than at any other time of my life and loved working the land. I had to make a living in town during the week but once I arrived home I was able to let it all go. There was always a project, inside or out. My garden was filled with delicacies and protected from the deer that ate everything else in the yard that wasn't fenced. We acquired two goats and named them *Mersi-doats* and *Dosi-doats* (no little lambs eating ivy). They were adorable and so entertaining. I loved Sundays. I'd get up early and make a bee line to the phone to call the local burn number. If it was a burn day (during the winter it usually was) I'd go out and get an early start on the week's worth of pine needles that I had raked from the lawn and covered to keep dry. Between the pine needles and all the pine cones it would make a nice hot fire. I gathered old wood from branches and debris throughout my property to stack on my fire pit specifically for these Sundays. By the late afternoon there were perfect coals beckoning a steak or hamburger for our dinner. We had a picnic table next to the fire and we would eat our dinner in the yard and watch the goats kick up their heals and run half way up a pine tree then drop to the ground and hook horns with each other as if they were jousting to win our applause! It was so much fun and our laughter encouraged them to do it all over again.

I originally wanted the goats so Nadia could participate in the local Pike school 4H program. Mersi was a brown and black LaMancha and Dosi was a white Nubian. Shortly after they came to live with us the 4H program became one of the many budget cuts and was eliminated. Oh well, they were a part of our lives now, and they had names, so they were there to stay. They made us laugh and they conveniently ate poison oak and manzanita. They didn't stop there of course; they also ate my roses, shoelaces and my hair when I was leaning over trying to clean their stalls. I loved them anyway. They preferred to be up in high places. I'd come outside from time to time and find them on top of the cab of the truck. I read in my *taking care of your goat* book that they are prone to a disease called enterotoxaemia, also know as overeating disease. I've had that before! It could be serious for goats though so I called our vet to inquire about the vaccine avail-able. She referred me to the only vet in the area that worked with small farm animals. Whenever I called his number for a time, I only reached his wife. She informed me that he was more of a traveling vet and hard to get a hold of. When I finally spoke with him directly he said Pike was too far to come. He wouldn't be able to bring the vaccines to me. He did offer a solution, however. Every Thursday he finished his day in front of a market on highway 49 toward the little town of Camptonville. It was called the *Golden Nugget* or *Little Nugget*, something with *nugget* in the name. What I do remember about this place is that it was in the middle of nowhere and located much further north as the crow flies, than Pike. It became a moot point. I was just happy that he offered to meet me at all. I was determined to get the vaccines and assure that my goats would remain healthy. Unfortunately, if he wasn't going to come to Pike and administer the vaccinations, that meant the burden was now on my shoulders to figure it out. His comment during the phone conversation when I sounded hesitant about my abilities to give the goats their shots was, "If you can't handle it then why did you get them in the first place?" I thought that was a rude and insensitive comment. I wanted to tell him I wasn't this blonde bimbo from the city that couldn't do things but remembered the old saying: *It is better to remain silent and be thought a fool than to open up your mouth and remove all doubt!* I'd figure it out. I always do. I got permission to pickup Nadia from school early that day so we could get up there to meet him by 4:00 or he'd be gone! I drove to this place that looked like a scene right out of the movie *Deliverance*. I told Nadia to stay in the car as I locked the doors behind me. I chuckle to this day at how out-of-place I must have looked in my dark plum business suit with black stockings and my black high heeled pumps. Of course he wasn't out front as he promised so I had to venture inside. It was dark in there, with neon *beer and bait* signs by a huge refrigerated section. I asked a couple of old guys, sitting around some tables, if the veterinarian that comes on Thursdays was still here. They both pointed to the guy standing in back. He acknowledged me with a question, "Are you the lady looking for the vaccines?" I whispered under my breath, *"No sh_t Sherlock"* and then replied with a polite, "Yes". We walked outside to his truck where he had my bag of syringes and vials of vaccine. I pulled cash out of my wallet and we made the exchange. It must have looked like an amateur drug deal going down to anyone watching from across the street. I laughed as I walked back to the car. My life seemed so funny to me at times. *Note to self: we should market this vaccine for humans.* Who wouldn't want a vaccine for our over eating during the holidays? Wouldn't that be great? Eat as much as you want over Thanksgiving and Christmas, then give yourself a shot on New Years and skip the whole dieting resolution thing. I went home to consult my goat **how to...**book to figure out how to give the Mersi and Dosi their shots.

There was a diagram in the book of a goat's loin. It showed right where the needle needed to go in. I wasted a precious vial by trying to stick Mersi with the needle with the vial attached. She immediately took off losing it all in the pasture. Wiser, the second time around, I stuck her with just the needle part. She took off but didn't lose the needle. It stayed intact long after she calmed down. Then Nadia and I went up to her nonchalantly with a handful of alfalfa and while she ate, I injected the vaccine into the needle. *Piece of cake.* I did the same for Dosi and we did high fives!

I had a great grandmother named Josephine on my father's side. She must have been the one I inherited the farming gene from, cultivating my need to be this pioneer woman conquering and taming the wild. As the story goes, Josephine's husband died at the age of fifty, leaving her with 10 children and a large cattle farm. She raised the family, tended to the farm and was ultimately appointed the first woman board member of the local bank. *Super Woman* of her day. I thought of her often as I dealt with challenges over those years. I kept her picture hanging in the hallway as a reminder that I could do anything I set my mind to.

I awoke one morning and went to the kitchen to get coffee. I thought it odd the cats were staring at the lower kitchen cupboards with way too much interest. I opened one of the cupboard doors and found mouse droppings all around the breakfast cereal and granola bars. That's also where we kept the cat and dog food. The bottom of the boxes had been eaten. Cereal poured out and the entire area was a big mess. I set traps with cheese and peanut butter and shut the cupboard after removing all the food and throwing it away. I wrapped rubber bands in figure eights around the cupboard handles to keep the cats from opening the cupboards and letting the mice escape. This didn't solve the problem. Somehow the mice were still getting in. I could hear them munching away at the *Captain Crunch* from my bedroom at night. It went on for months. I'd trap what I thought was all of them and once I put the food back, more would come! I was at my wits end and decided to get this figured out. I took everything out of the kitchen cupboards, took out the drawers, and even pulled the stove out from its space. That was the problem! Mystery solved! They were coming in from under the house through a vent hole which was square and the vent itself was round. There was enough room around the edges for the mice to fit. I got out my trusty duck tape, thank you *3M!* I used duck tape for everything back then, warts, leaky pipes, hoses with holes, insulating pipes in the winter and now mouse control. I put everything back one more time and felt certain it would be the last. One aggravation was over, but many more to come.

Growing up, I never really thought of water as a precious commodity. In Pasadena, it always came out of the faucet, even during storms. Same with the power, it was always on. Once in a while too many hairdryers and stereos tripped a circuit breaker but that was a quick fix. Not in Pike. The loss of both was inevitable and a *given* at the very suggestion of wind or snow. I was lucky enough to own a generator but that took some work on my part to assure it worked properly once it was needed. When I moved into the Pike house, I didn't know what a septic tank was. I didn't learn until later that you have to feed it like another pet, making sure it received regular doses of bacteria that eats the stuff that is flushed. I accidentally built my garden fence around the septic tank. In retrospect maybe that had something to do with quality of my soil and crop. I could have gone into the fertilizer business. It was important to always take care of your septic system. It was an expensive fix!

When we lost power, the pump to the well no longer worked. When the well didn't pump, there was no water, no toilet flushing and no showers. You get the idea. So I ran that generator religiously, every month to keep the battery charged and the engine cleaned out. I learned how to check the oil and clean out the little *filter thingy* on the side. I kept clean gasoline in the pump house and extra oil at all times.

Shortly after moving in, I was cooking dinner and noticed a light on in my pump house and a car idling nearby. I went out and found this man in there helping himself to my gas. He said, "I'm your neighbor and I needed gas. The last owners let me do this all the time by the way." "Yeah sure", I thought to myself. "Don't kid a kidder". The previous owners didn't live here full time. I suggested, as politely as I could muster up, that he ask me next time and proceeded to lock the pump house door with a padlock from that point on. He did ask a few more times and I finally resorted to lies, "I'm sorry, I only have enough for this one storm."

I was tired of being the only one around there that planned ahead! He was also the same neighbor I caught on my property one day, when I was home earlier than usual, trying to get his rickety old truck down to my pond to steal my row boat. He said it really belonged to him but he didn't get around to getting it back before I moved in. Who did they take me for anyway? The past owners never told me the boat didn't come with the pond. I told him he was trespassing and asked him to leave. I started locking all my gates to keep *the riffraff* out when I wasn't around. I'm sure the whole neighborhood was talking about me at the dump every week after that. The dump was like the water cooler in an office. It was where you heard about all the latest gossip about the town and its residents. The *transfer station attendant* as he liked to be referred as; was more informed about Pike business than the police blotter.

I had a system written out when we lost power. It was critical that before the generator was engaged, the power to PG&E (the power company) was off or it could injure one of the workers near the power lines. I followed these steps taped on my pump house wall. Once the generator was running, I stretched my 100 foot extension cord from it to the house in through the kitchen window. From that we would have electricity for the important appliances such as the refrigerator, the coffee maker and hairdryer. I would then notify PG&E on the non-portable phone kept for that purpose and push a series of numbers to let them know we were without power. I still have that number memorized! If no one notified them, we could be without power for days before they sent a repair person to the scene. Many of the residents in Pike were either retired or unemployed so they weren't as affected by an outage and never bothered to make the call.

One year we had a series of storms roll in, one after another. We lost power for a week and the phone eventually went out as well. We didn't get cellular service up there so we were really getting cranky. I had to get creative to locate someone in town who had a plow that didn't belong to the county and would be willing to plow the *non county* road. Everything was political, even in Pike.

I hadn't been to work and Nadia hadn't been to school for a week and we were tired of being poor shut-ins. I always kept cash stashed in the pocket of my grandmother's fur coat that hung on the coat rack by the front door for emergencies that required action. Cash made things happen up there! Our road finally was plowed. We could get back to civilization and the grocery store.

They Were the Best of Times and the Worst of Times

My daughter and I thought it odd when the neighbors (the same people who tried to make off with my boat and gas) asked Nadia to take care of their cat and two dogs when they went away on vacation. They said they would only be gone 10 days (a lie, by the way). They asked Nadia to come to their house and get instructions and they would pay her. She felt honored to be entrusted with this job. Little did we know that with their reputation and their animals' dispositions, no one else would accept the challenge! The first morning we went over to begin caring for these pets, the note left with instructions also informed us they would be back in 3 weeks! We called out "here kitty, kitty," figuring we'd take care of the cat first and then feed the dogs outside. No sign of kitty. We wandered to the back sun room where the litter box and food were. There were cat feces all around the litter box but none actually in the box itself! How odd. I started picking up the mess and tidying up a bit when Nadia screamed. The cat lunged out from under the daybed attacking her feet. This cat was no doubt possessed. It ran back in seclusion after the attack and refused to come out. I topped off the food bowl and changed the water bowl. I added new litter to the box hoping the cat would figure out what to do with it. My thoughts were interrupted by another warning from Nadia, this time on my behalf. Ouch! The cat scratched my ankles and got my tights in its claw. My tights immediately started to run and I could feel it go all the way up to my thigh. Great! I had no time now to go home and change. We were already running late and we still had to feed the dogs and put food out for the peacocks!! The dogs were a *piece of work*. We had no idea they had this horrible habit of chasing cars down the driveway. Another thing the neighbors conveniently failed to warn us about. We had no clue until now what we had taken on. There was no way Nadia could have done this alone. We tried to lock the dogs in this fenced area so we could at least get out of the driveway before they worked open the old broken down gate. It was a race for time. Each day, the getaway became more challenging but at least we came prepared in garden boots up to our knees to feed the cat. I installed a decent latch on their gate over the weekend to buy us some time with the dog problem dreading the fact that we still had over two weeks to go!

The following week, each morning ended the same, Nadia trying to make it into the truck before the dogs figured out how to get out of the fenced area and chase us. The new gate latch wasn't enough. The fence was so old there were many places to escape. It was obvious they had done this before. One morning, we weren't so lucky. I knew we were going to miss the bus if we didn't get out of there right now. I didn't want to step on the accelerator without the dogs in sight in my rear view mirror. By now we had turned off our dirt road onto the main paved highway, one of the dogs stayed at the end of the road, but the other was on a mission. I couldn't tell where he was, I asked Nadia if she could see him. She said "I see him". Then as I stepped on the gas she simultaneously said "now I don't". There was a thump...actually more of a thud and I looked behind me in the rear view mirror and he was lite*rally going in circles in the middle of the road like a* chicken with no head. My heart froze. Nadia said "Mom, I think we ran over his tail, we should go back". I couldn't go back and let her see what I feared we would find. I said, "There isn't time sweetheart, we'll go by the fire chief's house and ask him to help." I drove in his driveway in tears and he said not to worry. He would go back to see if the dog needed help. I said I'd pay for whatever it took to nurse him back to health if it wasn't too late. He said he'd call me at work with a report. I got the call. All he said was that the dog didn't suffer. He buried him on their property with his back hoe. Oh my God! I killed the neighbor's dog while they were on vacation. Who does such a thing? Certainly not me. And poor Nadia, she would feel so responsible. I woke up with nightmares every night, seeing the dog twirling in my rear view mirror. I was saddened by the circumstances but angry at these people for putting us through this. The day they came home I walked down to their house to explain why they had only one dog. They said, "Oh don't feel bad, it was bound to happen sometime. That dog loved to chase cars and bite at the car tires, we are glad to be rid of him. He was crazy anyway". I was devastated and wanted to strangle them all at the same time. They brought us both gifts from Bermuda and paid Nadia $40.00.

With regularity we brought friends of Nadia's up to spend the weekend. They would play dress-up and film their fashion shows, make up skits and in the wintertime, sled down the steep hill to our pond with boom box blaring. Since the nearest neighbors were twenty acres due south, they couldn't hear all the commotion. We never had to worry about disturbing anyone. I'd watch from the front porch with coffee in hand and wait until they came in soaked and cold wanting hot cocoa with marshmallows. We would drape all their wet clothes around the wood stove to dry for the next run. Life was good over those eight years, the happiest ever.

Nadia's birthday parties, which of course were overnights, were always well-attended because the girls were fascinated with the country life. It was different from their routine. I'll never forget her thirteenth birthday party. The girls awakened Saturday morning and wanted to take a Jacuzzi before breakfast. While I was making pancake sandwiches, they were in the hot tub on the back deck splashing around in the water, steam rising from the disparity between the temperature inside and out (it was January). My thoughts were suddenly interrupted by screams.

When I looked out the girls were all shivering on the deck and Mersi (the goat) was in the Jacuzzi! I ran out and pulled her out of the ninety degree water which was now filthy from her muddy hooves. I don't know who was more surprised, the girls or Mersi. The goats were used to jumping on top of the hot tub when it was covered. She didn't expect to land in water. If only I had been there filming it with a video camera. I could have submitted it to *Families Funniest Home Videos* and surely won the prize. The expressions on their faces were priceless.

No doubt about it, I was officially and completely *mountainized* (not a recognized word according to *Webster*). No *city* left in this girl. I drove a Ford F150 truck so I could bring alfalfa home for the goats and I often used it to move tree trunks from the back of the property up to the burn pile. It had a tow bar handy for up-rooting old fencing and t-posts which I'd dispose of at the local dump. I've never been in such good shape, physically as I was back then. My arms were buff and strong. I bought a chain saw and found lots of uses making the purchase worth it over the years.

A neighbor shared an interesting piece of news one day at the dump while I was unloading debris from my truck. He said, "Did you know the guys in town made a bet you wouldn't make it up here?" "Excuse me?" was all I said. I kept unloading my truck anxious to get out of there. "Yep, we placed bets on how long you and your daughter would tolerate this place and frankly we're surprised you've made it this long!" I got back in my truck and headed home remembering the different times I received calls from perfect strangers in the community asking for gas, inquiring if I would please drop their cat off at the vet and leave it, would I mind picking up flowers in town for their wife's birthday?, would I…? It went on and on. I guess the statement is true, *if you want to get something done, give it to a busy person.* That was me, the busy person people constantly asked favors of.

I tried to always plan ahead hoping to be prepared for the unexpected. It's how I was wired. I kept the pump house full of gas and oil all winter and the pantry full of food. When we lost our power, we'd try to make it fun by cooking spaghetti over the wood stove, playing *Monopoly* by candle light and listening to music on Nadia's pink boom box. We averted a potential disaster one evening during our candlelit *Monopoly* game, when Sassy the cat jumped on the table and her tail caught fire. She was very fluffy and as soon as I saw her tail touch the fire I grabbed it at the base running my fist straight up to the tip extinguishing the flame. She jumped down and looked at me in disgust as if to say in cat, *how rude*! Obviously, she was clueless to the fact we had just averted a disaster. We immediately extinguished the candles and turned on flashlights to finish the game. It stunk like burnt fur for a while. Whew, that was a close call.

Our generator had limited power. It wouldn't run the whole house at once so we learned to be selective with the things we needed at one time. On the weekdays the priorities included hairdryers, coffee maker, and the refrigerator. On weekends, we would fill zip lock bags full of snow and put them in the refrigerator to buy time and use the power for the TV so we could watch Sacramento Kings Basketball. We were die hard fans back in the 90s when they were winning. I got a super good deal on a hot pink 100 foot extension cord from the hardware store (no doubt because the color turned off most men). This pink cord ran from the pump house down to the house and up through the kitchen window for as long as the power was out, often for days. I kept a couple bags of cement in the back of the truck for the winter months. When it got wet and hardened and weighted down the bed of the truck so it didn't fishtail in the snow. I made certain to drive my truck around the circle driveway a few times, during the snow storms, to keep it packed down. We didn't want to get snowed in. I also kept a shovel, chains and jumper cables in the truck, just for precautionary measures.

I was constantly learning new things through trial and error. I had a well, and over time, the sediment in the well would cause the water from the washing machine to come out in just a trickle. Usually started with the hot side first. I thought there was something wrong with the washer the first time and called a service guy. After spending $100.00 just for the guy to show up, he located the problem. It was in the little *catch-all screen* filtering the water coming from the septic to the washer. It got plugged with sediment and he showed me how to clean it out. Once that was clean and flushed out, it worked fine. The rest of the time, I was able to do it myself avoiding a call. It felt good to be able to figure things out on my own and be handy. It was empowering, in fact.

We had numerous water leaks over the years. They scared me because of the amount of potential damage leaks could cause. I discovered the one in the wall behind the washer quite by accident when I walked over the wet carpet with bare feet in the adjoining room. I immediately turned off the main valve to the water for the house and called a handyman from up the road. His response was always the same no matter what the problem! "How soon do you need this fixed?" "Sooner than later would be great since we have no water!" He did everything in slow motion. I know that my high energy level got in the way of his yin and his yang.

That wasn't the only water disaster that almost happened. I recall another incident just before bedtime. Nadia was downstairs brushing her teeth and heard a strange hissing in the wall. "Mom"! She called out (in that voice that signaled to me something was about to cost a lot of money or make me really mad). I ran down and put my ear to the wall. It was a *water-leaking-hissing* sound inside the wall by her sink. I ran to the front door, flashlight in hand and put on that green and brown fleece jacket. It was after 9 pm and very dark. I needed to access the other side of that wall by crawling under the house. Sure enough, the red turn off/on valve for the sink in Nadia's room was spraying out a mist of water and it was running down the wall, forming a puddle just inches away from the nice new laminate floor we had just laid in her room. It was only the hot water leaking so we could leave the cold on. I got a mop and soaked up as much of the standing water as I could and connected a space heater for overnight to try to dry it out. I never knew the right name for things I needed at the hardware store. They were always so rude when I described what I wanted using words like *the turn on thingy*. My handyman would often scribble a shopping list on a piece of 2 x 4 with a broken pencil and say, "Go get this in town. The guys at the hardware store will understand what you need." Well, I'd go into the store and show them this list and they would invariably ask me questions I didn't know how to answer like "is it 5/8 inch or 1/2 inch, do you want galvanized or plastic?" How was I supposed to know? I'd get both to be on the safe side. It was a long way to have to come back if it was wrong. I made many, many trips down the hill for uninteresting things like nuts & bolts, galvanized pipe, insulation, you name it. It got *really old* after a while.

I celebrated my most memorable birthdays up there with Nadia and our friend. My presents from him included a shot gun, a vice for some of my projects in the garage and a set of jumper cables. All three gifts came in handy while living there. For the record, I never killed anything with that gun. I couldn't kill anything on purpose. I cried when I accidently ran over squirrels that often darted in front of my car. I did use the gun to scare a bear out of the yard one night and another time to keep a wolf at a safe distance once he killed our cat and chose to hang around and stalk us night after night. I was forced to carry that gun under my arm every time I went out after dark for protection, his beady eyes glowing in the dark, watching me. It was unnerving to say the least. It was up to me to protect my family and my animals. No one else! The gun offered me security.

No diamonds for this girl, I had a charge account at *Hills Flat Lumber* not *Nordstrom's*, like most women I knew. My gifts included things like muck boots, work gloves and a tool belt. For one of Nadia's birthdays, our friend had forgotten it was her birthday when we invited him for dinner. He rummaged through his pantry for just the right gift. He came down to celebrate this momentous occasion with a box of *Life Cereal* wrapped with elbow and wheel macaroni glued all over the box! She was thrilled! "The best gift ever", she exclaimed as she gave him a big hug. He never came to the door without flowers collected from the road along the way, sometimes even from my yard. It was the thought that mattered and in the winter he had to get pretty creative to even find anything blooming!

Christmas was my favorite time of year in that house. On December 1st, without fail, a local resident decorated each and every mailbox in Pike in the rain, snow, sleet, or sun. She would hang tinsel and one Christmas ornament on each box getting us all in the Christmas spirit. She'd take them down on December 31st. This tradition went on for the entire eight years we lived there.

The decorated mailboxes set the season in full swing for us. I would meticulously string lights along our deck and decorate the yard even though we were the only ones to really enjoy it. Choosing our tree was like a scene out of the *Chevy Chase* movie *Griswold Family Christmas*. We'd go out in the woods, often in knee deep snow where Nadia would select the ultimate Christmas tree for our home that season. She was very discriminate with her choosing and every year she would ultimately select the *perfect tree*. She and our friend would take turns using a hack saw to cut down the tree. No power saw for our old-fashioned Christmas tree! That would take all the fun away from the moment. I held the dog and captured each tree cutting ceremony on film for the scrap book that Nadia would put together marking another special year. We always had the same *Chipmunk Christmas* tape playing in the truck as part of the tradition with *Alvin* singing off key. One year we got all the way up to our parking spot to tree hunt, but no *Alvin!* We had to go back, fighting against darkness that year. No *Alvin*, no tree. Once we got the tree home, the two of them would work on the lights and decorations while I made a great meal. Times never to be forgotten.

Nadia gave me a book called <u>Bedside Prayers</u> by *June Cotner*, published by HarperSanFrancisco, 1997. It was a Christmas present to me while we were living in Pike. I keep it by my bed to this day and read it often for inspiration. The poem called *Testament* written by *C. David Hay* spoke to me as I began writing my own story.

"Life is an open book, a page turned every day,
We alone determine what the story is to say.
Some are tales of triumph, others wrought with woe,
All have the same beginning—the end we do not know.
Be the novel great or small, the paper is the same.
Its content is the measure, not the cover or the name.
Choose your message wisely, seek justice over wealth:
A classic for the ages—not dust upon the shelf.
When come the final chapter and the pen is laid to rest,
May God in final judgment say—we tried to write our best."
C. David Hay

Battling the elements was part of living in Pike. The snow, the rain and heat in the summer didn't really bother me. But the wind, that was a different story. The huge pines that towered over our property would sway back and forth as the wind literally howled through them. I'd lie in bed at night trying to cover my ears with the pillow to muffle the sound. The wind released the pine cones from the tops of these trees sending them down like torpedoes onto my metal roof making it impossible to sleep. I heard stories of trees crashing though houses, cutting them in half. At least Nadia was safe. I found comfort in the fact that her room was under ground level; the tree would only flatten me.

I must admit, the benefits of country living and rewards of living in Pike far outweighed the worries over water leaks, howling winds and power outages. I felt like I was continually creating a masterpiece, a painting, adding a little color here and there until I found perfection. I loved feeling so *at one* with nature and those incredible moon lit skies. It felt like God was watching over us in our own little corner of the world so far removed from reality.

After winter was behind us and all the bulbs pushed their way through the ground's surface announcing the arrival of spring. We started enjoying the outdoors once again. The evenings were longer and our croquet games resumed. Nadia loved to walk the goats on leashes to the mailbox at the end of the road and collect the mail with her Labrador retriever, Roxy, leading the way as her guardian. It was a sight that I will always hold close to my heart. She and her friends loved to turn on the sprinklers in the front yard wearing their bathing suits. They would carry umbrellas and dance around in the front yard. The goats delighted in this ritual running around locking horns and Roxy would bark out her orders as if she was in charge of all these shenanigans. We had a big tire swing in the front yard. The girls would swing from this tire or from the hammock that hung between two pines.

One of our croquet games almost turned deadly when we attempted to clear an area from pine needles and raked over an underground hornet nest. I didn't know bees made hives underground until then. Well, they were good and mad. They chased us all the way to the house, stinging me on the back of my leg, Nadia's arm and stinging the dog in a couple of places. It all happened so fast! I made a paste with baking soda and water and put it on our wounds. We were afraid to go outside. I phoned exterminators from the yellow pages. They all had the same response when I told them where I lived. "We're not licensed in Sierra County, sorry I can't help you!" I pleaded with one guy who seemed to at least be sympathetic to my plight. He finally gave in and said, "Alright, I'll come up and spray just this once but don't tell anyone I was there. I could lose my license for this." I convinced him his secret was safe with me. He arrived in a white suit covering his entire body with the head gear like that of a bee keeper. I felt like we were under quarantine watching him from our kitchen window. He waved and gave the *thumbs up* sign and drove away. That was the last of the bees and our croquet games were saved!

Living in Pike was supposed to be the simple life, not like a scene out of *Gunsmoke* or *Little House on the Prairie*. It was obviously different from city life and full of adventure but it also, more importantly, provided a wholesome, incredible life experience for Nadia while growing up. Thanks to living out *in the sticks* we were able to prolong her childhood and postpone the teenage drama that often sets in around thirteen. We weren't bothered by teenage boys covering our trees in toilet paper; no one could find us up there! Nadia learned the valuable lesson of being able to be content with herself. She enjoyed taking pictures and videos of her cat, Jules, all dressed up in *American Doll* outfits. She would videotape skits with her friends and then spend hours editing these creations, dubbing in music and sound on her Apple computer. Her movies always began with *Nadia Hitchcock Production* across the credits featuring her cat, Trixie yawning with the roar of a lion dubbed in.

Our first month living in Pike, my parents came to visit and celebrate Thanksgiving in our new home. Upon moving to Pike I thought it best to keep a low profile initially and get to know people in town on my own terms. It was Thanksgiving Day and the turkey was in the oven and I was ready to relax when dad announced that the toilet was stopped up. As a result, neither toilet was operable. What were we going to do? Nadia and I could use the great outdoors until I could get a plumber but not my dad and mom. I'm sure my parents could feel the tension as I was predictably freaking out! They excused themselves and said they were going to take a walk. I had given them the speech early in their arrival that I didn't want to gab too much with the locals until I had been there a while. I worried that the men up there might learn that a woman and her daughter were living alone and become a nuisance. Mom tends to say a bit too much at times and be over friendly so I gave them that speech along with the one about *less is more* when it came to toilet paper in the toilet due to our temperamental septic system. "It was better to flush twice", I tried to explain diplomatically, "than use too much paper all at once."

I was flipping though the yellow pages looking for plumbers when I noticed mom and dad walking back down the driveway, this time with a man I had never seen before. Dad introduced us when I walked outside, "Lisa this is your neighbor and the fire chief. I shook his hand and noticed he had some contraption under his arm. "This is a snake to clean out your septic and get it up and running again!" he said. I didn't know whether to be embarrassed first and then grateful or the other way around. "Don't you have something you'd rather be doing on Thanksgiving?" I asked. He said, "I'd rather do this than help my wife make a pie". He seemed totally serious. I didn't dare ask mom how this whole meeting and dilemma about our toilet problem became a topic of conversation. I just said thank you and had him show me where the septic pipe connected from the tank to our house for future reference. He found the clog and had it working in less than five minutes. Dad asked how much we owed him and he said $20.00 would take care of it. That wasn't the only time he would come to our rescue. Fire chief wasn't his only job. He worked for the county and plowed the main road during every snow storm. He knew we left for school and work early each weekday, so he made a point to start plowing from our end of town early so it was clear once we left. He also helped me remove a rabid bat that fell from my pump house door one day. I was concerned that my cats may mess with it so I covered it with an upside down trash can until he could come over and take it away. It was comforting to have him as one of my trusted *persons* to call on.

That following year, I hired his teenage son and his friend to do some clearing in the back of my property. It was the middle of summer and very hot. They told me they had found a nest of rattlers. "We killed them and disposed of the heads properly." I asked what *properly* meant. He explained that if you don't bury the heads, the hornets find them and suck the venom. The hornet then could sting one of us transferring the venom into our bloodstream. Good to know and good people to know. If you recall, this is the same family that came to my rescue when I hit and killed the neighbor's dog.

I think it's important to note here again, I really am an animal lover. I would never intentionally hurt any living creature. I sobbed all the way to work one dark morning after a deer literally fell from the sky and landed in front of my truck. I couldn't look back. It was too upsetting. I never got used to all of the road kill that we routinely encountered up there.

Now in the case of the mice, rabid bat and rattle snakes, these were situations where we just couldn't live harmoniously to-gether. One of us had to go. My wish was to be able to share the great outdoors harmoniously with God's creatures and we were successful most of the time. Just as a precaution and protection against human predators, I kept a pair of men's old boots and a big coat hung outside so it looked like a man lived with these two females just for piece of mind. Life in Pike was a peaceful, happy time overall!

We used the barter system up in Pike whenever possible and overall most of the people in the community were generally quite neighborly despite the isolated incidents shared earlier. When I moved in the previous owners said I could keep the ATV. The man of the house used it primarily to transport a 6-pack of beer to meet his old cronies at the back of the property. They would hang out and *shoot-the-breeze* until dusk drinking and smoking a little pot (for medicinal purposes of course). This was according to his soon-to-be ex-wife. She made him carry a *walkie talkie* so she could keep track of him once it got to be sundown. They left the communication device for us as well. Once back in Los Angeles they wouldn't have any use for either. I didn't really want the ATV or the *walkie talkies* but I needed gravel for my circle drive so I worked out a trade with the gold mine up the road. The miners were having difficulties getting trucks from one sec-tion of the mine to another so the ATV would be a perfect solu-tion. The mine had an abundance of tailings and crushed rock in piles everywhere. I had seen it spread out around the grounds. It was beautiful rock with shiny, glistening specks of crystal and gold-like flecks.

We worked out a delivery plan and finally one Friday afternoon the truck arrived with my rock. The miner brought it in two loads, dumping a pile at each end of the driveway. I hired the logger down the street to bring his loader over to spread it around the entire drive. By the time the sun began to set and it was all spread out I looked at this driveway covered with gray muck. Not the shinny, sparkling look I had bargained for. I called the mine phone and one of the miners answered. I expressed my concern that they had brought the wrong stuff. He assured me there was only one kind that they used for driveways. Oh well, it wasn't worth fretting over at this point. At least I had a driveway that wouldn't get muddy from the rain and snow anymore. I was too tired to fight it. It had taken almost a year for them to finally get it to me for one reason or another. The truck was either broken down or not street legal due to an expired registration. It was better than nothing at all. Just one more exercise in patience to add to my many while living in Pike. No one was in a hurry to do anything. I was, on the other hand, the *queen of hurry* and a *let's do it now* kind of person. It seemed futile up there at times and I was constantly reciting the mantra *just let it go*. It rained that night after the driveway was laid. In fact, it rained really hard all night. I woke to the sun pouring into my bedroom window that next morning and to my surprise and utter delight, when I looked out the window my driveway was transformed into a beautiful, white, glistening pathway. The rain washed away the muck and I had the most beautiful driveway in all of Pike! The miner was right! It was the good stuff. I felt badly for giving him a hard time.

I tried my hand at masonry, choosing the rocks by hand and loading them in the back of my pickup truck. There was an area between the ground and where my deck started and I wanted rock to fill this space. Not only did I think it would look nice but it would be functional as well. It would keep the critters from hanging out under there and replace the old, bug infested wood that was stacked there when I moved in. I made trips up to the mine in Alleghany and they allowed me to hand pick the travertine and quartz rocks perfect for my wall. I placed each rock meticulously against the next one, one by one fitting like a puzzle. I set each rock in mortar and cement. I was so proud with the way it turned out even though I suspect that project was the beginning of my chronic back problems. Whenever I made an appointment with my chiropractor, he would greet me with the question, "What did you do this time?"

Not to toot my own horn, but I also have an incredible eye for color. I painted each room of the house these beautiful warm greens, grays and slate colors. I learned to paint perfect straight lines where the ceiling met the wall. Masking off with tape didn't work for me. I have always been artistic, drawing and painting pictures for pleasure. This was just taking my creativity in a new direction and applying my talents to the walls. My home was truly a labor of love.

Those same miners helped me out another time when I was contemplating enclosing the area under my house and making it into a rumpus-type room, a place where Nadia could have friends overnight. This area under the house had a couple feet of dirt that needed to be excavated before it could be enclosed. I hired miners to dig out the remaining dirt with picks and shovels the old-fashioned way. Just as they worked in the underground mine every day, they hauled the dirt out by hand with wheel barrows. They were grateful for the pay and I was able to add an additional 700 square feet in that room alone. When we moved in, this area looked like it was a marijuana green house in the making, equipped with florescent lights hanging from the rafters and conveniently window free. It was now our great room with a big screen TV, a circular staircase going up to the main house and huge windows overlooking my massive Ponderosa pines. A room transformed into a spectacular vision. This room became Nadia's bedroom and a place where we spent many of our evening hours watching basketball games and giving each other manicures and pedicures.

One night, Nadia came upstairs and awakened me. "Mom, come listen to this noise in my room, I can't sleep!" She tried to describe this strange, scurrying noise in her ceiling as we came downstairs together. Sure enough, it sounded like a track meet for rats. They were running around the entire length of the room, back and forth. It was very disturbing indeed. I told her to come upstairs to sleep that night and I stayed awake most of the night trying to figure out how they got in there in the first place and how I was going to get them out!

I made a trip to my *not-so-favorite* hardware store and bought some traps. I crawled into that area under the house where I could access both the upstairs floor and the new room ceiling. Now you get why we named this place the *Money Pit*. This add-on took more money to complete than was in the budget! Anyway, back to the problem at hand. I found the spot where the wiring fed into the ceiling for the recessed lighting and I figured that must be where the rats were getting in and having their parties at night while we were trying to get some shut-eye. I carefully set the traps with peanut butter and cheddar cheese, a little trick I learned from my father. I carefully slipped the traps in through the opening and pushed each one back as far as I could reach aided by a yard stick. I had to be careful not to jiggle them as I pushed them back into the ceiling for fear they would snap prematurely. I closed the hole with small mesh chicken wire and hammered staples all around to fasten it to the 2 x 4s with no possibility of re-entry. Unfortunately I left out one very crucial step. I found this out the hard way. I didn't know you should always tie string to the end of the traps and secure the other end of that string to the entrance so they could be removed and discarded at a later date. The dead carcasses were left inside with no way to get them out! And to make matters worse, one of them didn't die right away and we had to listen to it dragging the trap around like a ball and chain. We felt terrible and to add insult to injury, once the noise stopped the horrible stench set in. At first it smelled like the cat litter box needed changing. Then we realized it was the smell of dead rats decaying in the ceiling (or the floor) depending on which level you were on. We burned incense for weeks trying to mask the smell but it didn't help much. The visual in my head of this massacre haunted me at night. It took over 3 weeks for things to get back to normal. Finally, no more rodents, no more noise and no more smell.

I often found myself lying in bed at night trying to differentiate the many different sounds of wildlife roaming the property in the night. This was the first place I had ever lived where there were no car noises, no street lights lighting up the sky, no sirens or noisy neighbors. I often questioned my sanity. What possessed me to move into this place in the middle of nowhere without a partner to share in the responsibilities? I was the sole provider of a ten year old daughter and tying to run a farm! What part of my past equipped me for this life? These *what ifs* constantly interrupted my sleep time! What if I got hurt and needed medical attention? How would we get down the hill to the hospital forty minutes away? Certainly not by calling 911! I knew the guys that would come. They hung out at the only bar in *Alleghany* or the *Brass Rail* down the hill. No thank you. I'd be safer putting my 10 year old behind the wheel! Besides, in a real emergency, I'd be dead before they got there. Because of the remoteness of our home, I made sure I was extremely careful when I would get into projects around the property that might be dangerous. I had to climb up on the roof to remove pine needles a few times each year. I'd let Nadia know that I was going to be up there and to please check on me. To my knowledge, she never did. The drop off at the back of the house was over three stories high because of the slant of my property. It wasn't the side I wanted to fall from. I also set the portable phone at the base of the ladder just in case. I never fell off but I had some close calls. Word to the wise, never get on a ladder wearing only socks! I was hanging curtain rods one day and didn't have shoes on. I thought I'd be fine climbing this ladder just this time without them. After all, I only needed to drill two small holes. Well, it was a near disaster. I slipped with the drill in my hand and fell onto my tailbone. The drill just missed my thigh and went straight into the wood floor with such force it impaled itself into the floor sticking straight up. It could have gone straight into my leg. I said a little prayer of thanks as I stood up unhurt and put my tennis shoes on to finish the job.

When we added the room downstairs, I added a trap door through the back closet into the garage for an escape route in the event of an uninvited intruder. This door led us into the garage where I always kept the keys in the ignition for a quick getaway. We never had to use it but it was a comfort nonetheless. This new room was a wonderful addition. It was closed off from the rest of the house by French doors and since it was partially underground, the noise stayed down there. Nadia had many slumber parties and overnights with friends, giving her privacy from me and vice versa.

We let our cats out during the day to enjoy the yard and all it offered but we brought them in at night and locked the kitty door to protect them from the wolves, foxes, mountain lions and bear that roamed after dark. When we came home on weekdays after school and work we often found the remains of critters that the cats would catch outside and bring through the kitty door as trophies to show off. We were constantly rescuing lizards with missing tails, birds without feathers, mice, moles and an occasional squirrel. Sometimes they were still alive so we'd spend whatever time it took to help them return to the wild. It was all part of country living. One real nuisance was this feral cat that adopted us and wouldn't go away. He started coming in through the cat door, eating our cat food and marking his territory. His foul-smelling spray lingering on our furniture and walls. It was time to take action. He was a huge cat, orange in color and obviously wild. Our cats hid whenever he came around. I went to *Ridge Feed* and bought a *Have a Heart* trap. These cages were a way of trapping something without bringing harm to the animal and gave you the ability to relocate them away from your home. One night we put the end of this trap up to the closed kitty door and draped a black sheet over it as a camouflage. The only part visible was the front opening. We put a piece of our salmon from dinner in the back and went to bed. It was a Saturday night. The next morning, around 6:00 I heard a noise, like a door slamming and then a growling sound. I jumped out of bed. It was barely light outside. I went out on the deck to confirm my suspicions, we had caught the cat! He was very mad. I went back inside to awaken Nadia. "Wake up sweetie, I need your help! We caught the cat and I want to let it out somewhere before everyone in the neighborhood gets up." I had already decided where I was going to take it and let it go. There was this beautiful meadow about 6 miles down the hill with lovely green lawn and cows grazing. With cows comes a barn, and with a barn there are rats. It was the perfect place to relocate our *friend*. Still in my pajamas I lifted this very heavy cage from the middle handle. The cat hissed and ran to one end and like a teeter-totter it fell to the ground. I would need Nadia's help and we'd better wear gloves. I found two pair in the garage and between us we got the cage into the back of the truck and headed down the hill, kitty howling all the way. I turned onto *Celestial Valley Road*, the location of this farm and told Nadia she'd better stay in the truck in case he tried to retaliate. I tipped the cage down toward the road from the back of the truck bed (still in my pajamas mind you) and opened the door. It was really strange. After jumping to safety onto the road below he stopped, and turned around to look at me. I like to think he was saying *thank you* but it could have also been his way of saying "if looks could kill, you'd be dead lady!" He never came back to bother us again so life must have suited him there. I never needed that cage for anything else. I was glad.

There was always something needing my attention around there. We found termites in the garage, rattlesnakes living under the deck by our pond, raccoons raiding the compost pile, deer eating my rose garden and the huge hawks that would circle over my cat, Sassy, contemplating whether she would be worth the fight. I look for a stone to throw in the hawk's direction to distract it. If I could catch Sassy I'd put her inside whenever possible. She is the only cat from Pike that is still with us today. The others weren't so fortunate. Our beloved Jules had a heart defect and I found her one day in a pile of fluid slowly dying a painful death while Nadia was at *Great America* for an eighth grade year end excursion with her classmates. I called the vet begging them to stay open until I got there and I headed down the hill, Jules crying in pain the whole way. I kept telling her to hang on, she would be alright; alright that is until I spotted the familiar light blue Nissan truck ahead. Oh no, not now. I was behind this older couple who we encountered at least once a week in their dilapidated truck.

Of all days to get behind them! The wife always drove and the husband sat in the passenger side hooked up to oxygen tubes. They never drove more than 15mph down the hill and it was a narrow, divided road that wound all the way to town offering no passing lanes. Their faded blue pick up truck had a bumper sticker that read: *Run like a Deer.* How ironic. There was nothing deerlike about the way they traveled. I was desperate and had no choice but to pass them on the right when an opportunity opened up. I had to get down that hill to help Nadia's precious kitty. I arrived at the vet office before they closed. He took very little time to assess her condition. The humane thing to do was to have her put to sleep. I was devastated. She was the love of Nadia's life. I gave my consent through my sobs and Jules was finally free of pain. The vet tech put her back in the box I brought her in and they covered her with her pink blanket that I had knit when I was a young girl for my kitty, Muffy. I called my friend in tears and asked him if he would help me dig a hole to bury her in my garden. He dug a very good, deep hole. He had tears in his eyes too. We left the grave uncovered so Nadia could pay her respects and add some of Jules favorite things to be buried with if she wanted. Nadia was overcome with grief when she got home from her long day. She was so upset she couldn't bring herself to attend her 8th grade graduation ceremony that night at school. We just stayed home and talked about what a great kitty Jules was.

We had another cat by the name of Trixie who wasn't very nice. We had re- named her *Large Marge* after a radio celebrity because she was such a big, cranky, old tabby cat. She was the *alpha cat* who picked on Sassy who in turn picked on Jules. That was just the way it always played out. Jules was Nadia's cat and Sassy was mine. Trixie was boss of all of us. Jules always stayed very close to Nadia, allowing her to dress her in doll clothes posing for many pictures. They were quite a pair. Trixie was a loner and loved to hunt things during the day and sit inside on the back of a chair at night and be grouchy. Once Jules died, there was an interesting transformation that came over Trixie. We believe Jules was so worried about how Nadia would take her death and how sad she would be, she switched souls with Trixie. Jules' soul lived in Trixie from that day on. Trixie became a different cat and took on the role of comforting Nadia during her time of sadness. She became Nadia's bed partner and even took on Jules' sweet demeanor. It was quite a transformation. I planted daffodil bulbs over Jules' grave and each spring the beautiful yellow flowers reminded us of just how lovely she was and how blessed we were to have had her for that brief time. Unfortunately before we moved from Pike, Trixie was attacked in broad daylight, by the wolf that had become a nuisance throughout the neighborhood. She was plucked from her front yard where she loved to sit and enjoy the sun. We found her collar and blotches of her hair around the yard after work one afternoon. Something inside of us died with Trixie that day. The love of the wild lost its luster for us after that. I had to carry my shot gun just to take the dog out to go potty at night. I felt stalked by this animal who was ruining our quality of life. I couldn't bear to lose another animal. The idea of anyone else dying right now was just too painful. I shut the kitty door for good.

Sassy was a pound kitty. She chose me. The night before this union, we had our friend to dinner and as usual we were setting up the croquet game when Nadia came running over reminding him there was a cat in a cage in the back of his truck. He said he had forgotten about it (truth be known, he knew we were suckers for wayward cats needing a meal). It looked really ratty, like it hadn't had a meal in a very long time, but had a very sweet face. Nadia said "Mom, can we keep him, pleeease?" I replied, "You can feed it and keep it under the house for the night (the new room wasn't built yet) but we'll need to get it checked out by a vet before it can be around Trixie". She named it Lucky. Big mistake! The cat stayed under the house. It was well fed, kept warm with a doll bed and given lots of attention all evening. Next morning, I put Lucky in the cat carrier and after dropping Nadia off at the bus stop, I left him at the vet for a check up. The last thing Nadia said when she got out of the car was, "Mom, can you come get me from school today and bring Lucky with you so I can show my friends?" I said "OK" with some hesitation. I got the vet's call around 10:30 that morning while I was at work.

He said Lucky was a very sick cat. Not a lucky cat after all. He explained that Lucky had a number of issues, including a bowel obstruction and distemper. The cat wouldn't be able to live a quality life and the humane thing (again) was to put him to sleep. I felt terrible. Tears ran down my cheeks as I gave him permission to put the poor cat down. I couldn't risk making our cat sick too. Then I made a plan. If I had to take a life today, I was going to save one. I left work early and went to the animal shelter in town. There were two tabby female cats in one cage together. I picked up the first one and looked at her face. All I could think about was replacing Lucky with a cat in time for school to get out. Then the other female in the cage made a point to get my attention. I don't remember if it was a meow or a paw in my direction but I looked at her and put the other one back. I'll take her, this one. Her name was to be Sassy. She hated the cat carrier right away so I took her out and put her in my lap as I drove to Nadia's school. She was so tiny and cute with these big blue eyes. I waited for Nadia to come out to the car, Sassy still sitting in my lap. Nadia came running to the car, "How's Lucky?" After explaining how sick he was and how she had given him the best 24 hours of his whole life, her tears stopped flowing down her face as I handed Sassy to her. At home, Trixie wasn't very receptive to the newcomer but they eventually worked out their differences as most cats do. However, Sassy and Nadia never really bonded. The bond was always between Sassy and me from the very start. Right after adopting Sassy, Jules adopted us (a stray from Alleghany) and you know the rest of that story.

To this day, Sassy remains the queen of our household. She is eleven now but still looks as young as she did when she was a year old. She sleeps with me every night and sits on my computer keys when I'm trying to work. I kiss her face and shower her with love. We've been through so much together. It's what we do, treat all of our pets as members of the family and as a result they have brought us a lifetime of pleasure, each and every one. Sassy is strictly a house cat now. After living in Pike she has no doubt used up most of her 9 lives. So I don't want to take any chances.

Must Get Out!

Nadia and I were both getting restless even prior to the Trixie incident. It was soon after her junior year in high school we were on the brink of needing change. The trees sensed this change as the wind shifted directions and started to blow. The weather was turning and skies getting dark. I braced myself for the inevitable. Nadia fueled the change by turning into a full blown teenager overnight. I was fortunate that it was late in coming. Other mothers had been complaining about their teenage girls for the last couple of years. Nadia suddenly resented being away from the *fun* when she entered high school. She referred to Pike as the time when she had *no life!* She hated everything about where we lived. She hated me for subjecting her to it. She was argumentative and challenged everything I stood for. There was distance building between our friend and me. She blamed me for that as well. She was too young to understand that I felt I deserved a commitment and *more* out of a relationship. Nadia didn't understand why I couldn't just be happy with things the way they were. I was approaching my fiftieth birthday and I too, started getting restless. It hurt me to see my daughter this way but friends assured me that the pulling away was just her way of spreading her wings and showing some independence. I felt abandoned and feared life was passing me by. Was I really about to be fifty? Where had the time gone? My daughter hated me and the guy in my life didn't care enough. Fifty represented this deadline that was going to come whether I was prepared or not. I began focusing on what I didn't have. I thought I needed a commitment from the man in my life when I really should have been counting my blessings and embracing what I did have. I was at a point where I was tired of handling every crisis alone. I had been in *fight or flight* mode for so many years I wanted to slow down and find a place where things didn't break and life wasn't so hard. I was trying to control a life that couldn't be controlled. There are people out there that aren't the *settling down* type. They can't be *owned or fenced in* as *Willie Nelson* sang in one of his songs. I stopped sleeping (a symptom of worry and anxiety) and started stressing over future events such as Nadia learning to drive on those horrible roads and all the repairs that were going to be needed on this house soon including a new deck. Money was tight, always tight and one thing always led to another more costly problem. I felt like the very place that had brought me such joy, initially was now sucking me dry. I envisioned Nadia driving in another year and trying to get to school on that road, winding along cliffs and how I'd feel every morning waiting for that call that she had made it safely to school. I prayed for guidance and got the answer on the drive down to work that next morning. I said out loud in words that didn't sound like my own, "I'm going to sell the house." Nadia did a double take, not sure whether to take me seriously. She said nothing in reply. I called a realtor by noon and the *For Sale* sign went up on Labor Day weekend. We had been there eight years. What ever I needed to prove, I proved it! It was time to go. After making the decision that day, I walked around my front yard stomping down the mole holes, crying. I would really miss so many things about the place. I had learned so much and had become so competent at fixing leaky sprinklers, working handily with power tools and fighting off the wild life. We had made memories that no one could take away. After the house fell out of escrow twice and more things began needing repair, it was now clear to me that it was time for us to go. It was a sign from God that we were ready to move on to our next chapter in life. Nadia was already distancing herself from me and planning her life away from here after high school. If I was going to be alone, I didn't want it to be living in Pike, that's for sure.

Finding Freedom!

One Sunday morning on our way to church we passed a house under construction with a *For Sale* sign in front. It was in downtown Grass Valley. "Mom stop!" Nadia cried. I looked at the house she was pointing to, an old Victorian obviously under renovation. The door was propped open with a bucket and *wet paint signs* posted. We decided to trespass since no one answered our **hello** calls. When we walked through the front door, it felt like home. We both felt it. Nadia looked happier than I had seen her in months. We walked around the mess, nothing really finished, no fixtures, no appliances, but the foundation and floor plan was perfect for all my 1930s furniture that belonged to my grandfather and grandmother. It was strategically located within walking distance to town on a street in historic Grass Valley appropriately named *Main Street*. It couldn't have been any more different from the life we were leaving. Maybe that was part of the appeal. From twenty acres to a quarter acre, it felt like the right *next step* for us. The back yard had two apple trees and enough area for an herb garden. That was actually a manageable size. This house had good energy. It was built in 1898, the year my grandmother was born. My roots were also traced back to here, a distant relative who had a shoe repair business around that time in Grass Valley, on South Auburn Street, just blocks from this very house. We put an offer in on the house and it became ours. We were convinced this was *home* beckoning us to make the leap of faith.

We moved in November, 2005. Nadia pleaded with me to get rid of all my Pike work clothes. She said now that we lived in town I shouldn't be seen in those converse tennies held together with duck tape and that green and brown fleece jacket I loved so much. I didn't want to embarrass her so I did as she asked. I regretted not saving them for a good laugh. I should have at least kept the net headdress and pink scarf ensemble just as a reminder of where I came from!

We sat there in my bed room, in Pike, ready to take the last load down the hill. All that was left was a box of miscellaneous cleaning supplies and our Sassy cat. Obviously impaired by her memories of life in a cage at the pound, Sassy didn't do car rides and kitty carriers with dignity. Typical behavior when subjected to car rides caged in resulted in serious howling. She would ram the cage door with her nose until it would start to bleed. We couldn't let her loose in the car or she would jump from window to window with her paws on the automatic window button causing the windows to come down offering her a potential escape. In anticipation of this upcoming forty minute car ride to the new house we invested in drugs. The vet called them a *kitty cocktail* just to take the edge off. We gave her one, shoving it down her throat while she fought with all she had and then we waited. We sat on the carpet, since all the furniture was in a moving van and we watched Sassy get more and more friendly kissing the walls, kissing the closet door, even rubbing against Nadia as if they were suddenly best friends. It was quite funny. But after forty-five minutes she didn't look the least bit sleepy and we were getting impatient. The vet said it would take effect by thirty minutes. We gave it an hour. It was now almost dark and we were anxious to leave Pike and move into our new home. Enough of this waiting, maybe she would fall asleep once in the carrier. Wrong! She started wailing, unaffected by the drugs. We had no choice but head down the hill and tolerate it. Nadia tried to keep Sassy's head away from the carrier door and avoid getting bit at the same time. We turned onto the main road, leaving Wild Rose Meadow Lane for the last time passing the local guys playing horse shoes, a Friday night ritual with their 24-pack of beer in tow. Nadia's comment was classic as they all waved good bye, beer in hand, "I bet they are saying, there goes the only real *class act* this town has ever known". I chuckled and thought to myself, yes it's true, we brought class to this town but this little town of Pike didn't need us as much as we needed this place. We were better for the life lessons we learned here. Pike would always be Pike. It was a necessary chapter for our personal growth and building strength of character. Pike gave both of us important tools for the future. Sassy fell asleep once we arrived in Grass Valley. The ride exhausted her, not the drugs. In retrospect, we should have saved the drugs for ourselves after enduring the forty minute ride in the car with her. We were the ones who desperately needed that *kitty cocktail!*

Selling the chateau in the woods didn't go as smoothly as hoped. We were in escrow when we bought the Victorian named *Freedom.* Unfortunately over Thanksgiving, a week after moving in, I got the call from the realtor, the prospective buyers for Pike backed out. They got cold feet. Yikes, I now owned two houses, two mortgages and taxes on both properties for an indefinite period of time. I tried not to panic which is often what I do when I feel overwhelmed. I tried not to think negatively about going into the winter season when no one typically looks for houses, especially with the upcoming holidays. It immediately put a dark cloud over the euphoria I had felt just the day before about living in town and embracing my new home. It was hard not to be worried. I did get a call a few weeks later from my realtor saying two couples were at my Pike house looking with some interest in possibly buying it as a retreat. Since I had learned that realtors are masters at making an idle inquiry into a buyer I didn't want to get my hopes up. But one afternoon while I was at work, my realtor's assistant said there was a lady from Reno who wanted to see my place. She didn't have a broker to escort her. Could I meet her there? What gall! My broker was never there again once I signed the papers authorizing the full commission. It was convenient for me to show my own house while we were living there but now I couldn't just take off from work and go up with out notice! The broker's assistant asked, "Would it be alright with you if we let this woman know where the key was hidden and let her go through the house alone? I checked out her website and she looks trustworthy." I pulled up her website on my computer, she was a photographer and her photographs were beautiful, mostly of children and animals. She was pictured with her dog and looked lovely. Supposedly she and her husband were looking for a home with property and she wanted to look at my house today. I gave my consent and told her the key was hidden in the jar inside the garage door. Little did I know that this was a miracle in the making and the answer to all my desperate prayers! Little did I know I had just given permission for my *Guardian Angel* to go to Pike? She went to look at my house that afternoon and it just so happened the other people, the two couples considering this property for their retreat, were out there as well walking around the property. They felt pressure now with this new person interested. Just the competition needed to get them off the dime. They immediately called my broker to inquire as to how much time they needed before putting in their offer? My realtor said we would consider what ever offer was submitted first. The next morning the two couples offered the full price (which was higher than the other past two offers) and we never heard from the photographer from Reno again. She disappeared. I tried to go back to her website to thank her for visiting and to save her picture for a scrap book but I couldn't find that either. The important thing was, we were back in escrow and my prayers were answered! I called my parents to share the good news. My mother had just finished polishing spoons. She said, "You remember those spoons don't you, Lisa? The ones I inherited from your grandmother's collection of silver demitasse souvenir city and state spoons?" I said "yes". I always reply "yes", when she asks, "do you remember?" I never want her to think there are times I'm not really paying attention to what she was telling me. "Your grandmother loved to collect these spoons when she and granddaddy traveled to different cities and states over the years." I guess that was the thing to do back then, collect spoons for tea. Mom went on to explain that she had just finished polishing each one by hand and meticulously put them away for later use when I called. Mom has quite a collection of silver and china tea sets and place settings so it wasn't unusual for her to be spending her time polishing all of her pieces. What was unusual though was that during our conversation over the relief we all felt about my house being back in escrow, my mother moved papers on the table where she had polished the silver and a single spoon had been overlooked and fell to the floor…"oh no, I missed one" she said in the phone. "Well, would you look at this?"

"What mom?" "Here is the work of your angel, sweetheart, this spoon is inscribed with the city name **RENO**". We both got goose-bumps. She polished it and sent it to me. I currently have it displayed on a plaque I made with angel wings and the following inscription:

"We each have an angel sent from Heaven above. She keeps us safe and guards our life, giving guidance mixed with love. If you listen very closely, you'll hear whispering voices sing and for heavenly comfort every night, she tucks you peacefully under her wing."

We closed escrow, for good, just before Nadia's seventeenth birthday. Unfortunately for them, the new owners put the Pike house back on the market not long after that. Sierra County wouldn't allow them to make all the changes they wanted for their retreat. As far as I know it sold again but no one lives there now. The owners supposedly live in Brazil. I can't bring myself to go to Pike and possibly ruin this *visual* I still have of our beautiful green lawn and the gazebo we built by the pond. Our big, blue bass fish named Beans lived in that pond and would come to the surface when we offered handouts of fish food. The pussy willows which surround the waters edge and served as a hiding place for these cute little birds that we named Ocello. They had the sweetest song and renewed our friendship each season when they came back to visit. The pier was a favorite of Nadia and her friends, where they stretched out and worked on their tans, music blaring over the boom box. No, I can't go back, I couldn't bare to see it in a state of disrepair.

Once I got into town I tried dating again. It seemed so foreign. The men appeared ordinary, shallow and needy. They'd always ask the same question as an ice breaker, "What do you like to do for fun?" After these past 8 years in Pike I had no idea how to answer that question. I missed the relationship with my guy up in Sierra County. But, we weren't able to take it to the next level so it had to end. On top of my bad dates, Nadia's senior year was extremely difficult for me. She was in rebel-mode. She lied to my face and caused me many a sleepless night. "It's all part of growing up" my sympathetic friends and co-workers would say. I had hoped we were different. We had just postponed the inevitable and I got hit with it all at once in her senior year. I likened it to a mother bird pushing her baby out of the nest to fly except in our case I was the one being pushed out. Nadia didn't want to need me. She kept saying, "I can't wait to get out of here and go away to school." Her plan was to go down to southern California and live with her dad and attend community college in Orange County. I had planned a trip to Italy for her graduation gift, just the two of us. There were moments during that year when I thought seriously of going on the trip alone sending her south saying, "Good riddance and don't let the door hit you on the way out!" It was just me feeling hurt and rejected. We went on the trip and had the time of our lives.

After reading the inspirational book <u>*Under the Tuscan Sun*</u> by *Frances Mayes* and then going to the movie of the same name staring *Diane Lane* (released on my fiftieth birthday) I was bit by the *Italy bug* big time! The breathtaking scenery in that movie inspired us to choose Italy as our destination for our mother-daughter trip. We arranged to spend most of the trip in Sorrento and Positano and Capri on the Amalfi Coast and reserved the last two days for Rome and shopping for *i tacchi*, (Italian for high heeled shoes). The Italian men were taken by my daughter's beauty. It's ironic since almost eighteen years to the day we had been in Italy on a trip along the Mediterranean Coast with her father and his parents. Nadia was only 9 months old at the time. I was very protective then just as I was this trip but for such different reasons. My father-in-law enjoyed tormenting me on that first trip. He warned me that in Italy the Gypsies had a reputation of stealing young children. I wouldn't let Nadia out of my sight for even a minute and it put a damper on the trip for me. Now after all these years, back in Italy, every man's jaw dropped when she walked down those cobblestone streets! It wasn't the Gypsies I worried about this time. I insisted she always walked in front of me on those narrow streets through the piazza, again not letting her out of my sight! The trip was good for us both. We were able to leave the mother-daughter conflicts behind and enjoy each others company as travel companions for those two glorious weeks. Filled with unforgettable memories, we returned carrying a little bit of Italy home with us in our hearts.

I must admit, hardly a week goes by when I don't reflect on those days in Pike and marvel at what I was able to accomplish, equipped initially with so few skills. It was mostly due to dumb luck at the beginning, living off the land and dodging the many curve balls thrown my way. I often asked myself, why a girl from the city, in her right mind, would seek that kind of life for herself and her young daughter. Looking back, I believe that was the *real* me up there. The Lisa I was in search of. Yet I left it because I got tired of being alone and could project into the future just how much worse it would feel once Nadia moved out. I was searching for a relationship that could offer me more. I wanted security and stability as I entered my fifties. I was afraid of getting old. The same way I felt in my twenties when I felt pressured to marry the first time. I thought I was getting old then, at twenty-five. What was I thinking? I long for the relationship my parents have. I know, it's too late to have fifty-five wonderful years but I could conceivably have twenty with someone. I think it is the Pasadena influence. I long for the traditional family life I had growing up. Even though I didn't exactly follow in my parents footsteps embracing the game of bridge or the musical instrument thing (I quit playing the piano as soon as I left for college), I did inherit their ethical standards to always *do the right thing in all circumstances* and unconditionally love your children. My parents weathered their storms of life together and came out stronger and more in love than any couple I know. I admire that and am envious in a way. I feel pressure on the one side to try to seek that kind of love yet fear that I may be too set in my independent ways to compromise at this late stage of the game. Nadia said to me the other day, "Mom, I can't see you ever getting married again. You don't do change well! Remember when I lived at home and I moved something from its proper place. You hated that! How are you going to tolerate the same if a man is living in your house?" She's probably right. She knows me so well. I need to mindful of what I wish for. It might come true and may turn out to not really be my wish at all.

Our childhood was for wishes, believing in that bucket of gold at the end of a rainbow and that our prince will ultimately ride in on his white horse. Eventually life snaps us into reality. I want to go back to those lazy summer afternoons when my sisters and I had run out of things to build or create and we would saunter down to the park at the end of the street to spin around on the merry-go-round. We didn't have to talk. I always took my usual position on top of the center pole and my younger sisters, Lori and Lynn, liked to hang on at the outer edge and take turns pushing it really fast and then at the last minute, jump on. They would laugh as we would spin round and round getting dizzier than I, which seemed to be their favorite part. I remember how it felt to gaze up at the sky at the tree tops watching the world spin around feeling an unexplainable peace, perched in the center of it all. I was in control of my universe for that brief moment. But in keeping with the expression, *all fun things must end*; my euphoria was often interrupted by neighbor boys. They would show up and start spinning us so fast that my sisters would end up in a heap in the sand, unable to hold on under the duress. I had no choice but to stay put and ride it out. I learned that if I didn't yell for them to stop, they usually lost interest and allowed the thing to slow down enough to hop off and go home. Boys grow up to be men eventually, or do they really?

Why do we have to lose our childhood innocence? What happens to our belief in the *tooth fairy* and *Santa Claus* and a *happily ever after*? When I was 7, I dreamed I could actually fly. I dreamed this dream so vividly; I still remember it to this day. I got up on my bed like *Sally Field* in the *Flying Nun* and caught a draft. I started flying effortlessly around the room. It felt glorious! I tried to describe the feeling to my parents, how real it felt to me and that anything is possible! Of course they wouldn't play along with such nonsense. They squelched my enthusiasm and made me feel silly for believing in that which is unseen or believed to be impossible. Dreams were for underachievers and I had chores to do. What about faith and believing in God? Untouchable, yet real to us just the same. As grownups we should try to hold on to our childlike beliefs into adulthood and our abilities to fly and do the unimaginable. We need to hang on to those whimsical times of our youth. As adults we get wrapped up in the reality of our day-to-day lives and miss out on what is really important. It is not about the fancy vacations and exclusive golf memberships. It is not about the dinner at a restaurant that costs an obscene amount of money. It more about fireflies in a jar on a balmy Kansas night when we would make family trips to visit our grandparents. It is about that tooth under the pillow and a hole in your daughter's mouth where that tooth was just hours ago. It is sharing in the excitement and expectation of the tooth fairy coming and scrambling through your wallet while your daughter is sleeping hoping to find coins to slip under her pillow before dawn. It's your sleepy cat spread out on the outfit you just laid out on the bed to wear to work and you decide on something else because you don't want to disturb her. It's putting service before self when you help an elderly person carry his or her groceries in the house while you're on your daily walk or buying the homeless man a gift certificate from *McDonalds* and seeing his toothless smile. What has happened to our world? Why do we fight and complain so much? We're all living under the same moon that light up our same skies every night. We are so busy on the fast track of life that we forget to get off and savor these things. I want more dreams of flying and less about destructive ball machines.

I used to complain about the messes my daughter made when she lived at home, hair in the bathroom sink, the bathroom always in disarray and her room a disaster. I would give anything to have my Nadia in her room right now, her music blaring and her messy ways. She is away now and I'm hanging on by a financial thread tying to pay her expenses along with my own in a plunging stock market and tumbling real estate values. Our world is in turmoil and the *forward thinkers* in history must be shaking their heads. My grandfather was one of those men. He ran a profitable business with a handshake through acts of kindness throughout his lifetime. He was always true to his word. He would have been appalled at the greed and corruption that runs rampant in our business world today.

Our political parties have never been so divided and we still aren't very accepting of other races, religions or beliefs. The baby boomers have been followed by the *entitlement generation*. Too much *all about me* thinking and not enough regard for others. We are a long way away from embracing the *one in the same concept* and women are working harder than ever; often more than one job, just to put food on the table. The unfortunate part is the fact that women are a long way from getting paid for their worth and aren't close to getting the same pay as their male counterparts. It is still commonplace for women to be discriminated against and harassed in their workplace. In my career I have hob-knobbed with the *good old boys* who didn't turn out to be good or very nice. Often times we are afraid to make trouble for fear of losing the job we need so badly. Then we get into our late forties and early fifties, after all the sacrifices we've made over the years, only to be cast aside and passed over because now we're old and a liability as far as benefits go. We need to get out there and be heard. What was the name of that movie where the guy yelled out the window, "I'm mad as hell and I'm not going to take it anymore?" Sometimes I feel like screaming those very words to anyone who will listen.

I was reading the headline in MORE magazine while waiting in line at the grocery aisle a few months ago. It's the only time I read a magazine anymore (oh, and maybe at the dentist office twice a year). There was an article about this very subject I'm talking about. It was a quote from a NYC freelance writer by the name of Amy Engeler.

"For a generation of women who witnessed historic strides in abolishing discrimination based on race, religion, disability, sexual orientation and yes, gender, it can be almost impossible to fathom that they might now be getting pushed out simply because they have reached a certain age. But recognizing an inequity is always the first step in resolving it..."

This was exactly the point I've been trying to make. Another headline in the same magazine read: *Why smart men have stupid sex*. It was a great read! It was called <u>MORE</u>, the 10th Anniversary November, 2008 edition featuring *Jane Fonda, Sharon Stone and Tea Leoni* looking gorgeous on the front cover sharing secrets on how they have reinvented the 70s, 50s and 42 and breaking the age barrier. Easy for them to say, they are famous and beautiful. In that article about the stupid sex and stupid men entitled *Sex, Lies and Trouser-Gate, Why Smart Men have Stupid Sex?* It simply reinforced and validated so much of what I have experienced over the years. I was encouraged by the validation that I wasn't alone. Although with most of the men who have behaved badly throughout my career, I wouldn't give them credit for being that smart! I've been hit on, propositioned, harassed, whatever name you want to give it by married neighbors, married fathers of my daughter's friends, married members of my church, married bosses, married co-workers, and married clients. It's been hard not to be angry and bitter at times. The magazine was confirmation that we have more work to do if we are going to be successful in moving out of the dark ages.

As mothers of daughters and sons, we have an obligation to teach our children and grandchildren that this is not OK. It's wrong to passively sit back and be victims. We all know we are the stronger and smarter sex and the masters of multi-tasking. After all, God chose us to bare the children, act as caregivers, chauffeurs, chefs, warriors and protectors, referees, confidants and when the kids are at school, we go to work. Can you see men going through 9 months of pregnancy with morning sickness and hormones raging out of control? Most can't even have a head cold without whining.

Insomnia

It is a fact of life for me these days. Sleepless nights, tossing and turning, trying to solve the day to day problems when I'm supposed to be sleeping and preparing myself for the next round. If I were to chart my sleep patterns, it would resemble that of the S&P 500, choppy and volatile. I'm afraid I've managed to manifest the very life I feared most. I've tried to make a living in this world of finance and have done right by my clients. However, I have moved from firm to firm when men in the office made it impossible for me to stay. No matter what impression you have of me so far, I'm not a fighter. I really don't like conflict. I know that some women have sued the companies they have worked for, and taken their harassment gripes to the top of these corporations and lived the rest of their lives, comfortably due to the settlements they received. Maybe I should have joined them and held my greedy Wall Street employers accountable for their bad behavior to pay for my pain and suffering. But I didn't choose that path. I moved from one boiling caldron to the next.

I have tried all kinds of over-the-counter remedies that guarantee a great nights sleep. So far they all fall short. After all, my nights are reserved for worry and hot flashes these days. It's just the way it is. We no sooner get rid of those pesky menstrual periods and we start sweating like a swamp cooler. With no warning black facial hairs start growing in places we never thought possible and our arms get shorter when we try to read a book! The hot flashes are worse at night so I run the ceiling fan, even in the winter. The cats have compensated by growing heavier coats than usual. I wake up with my heart pounding, worrying about everything under the sun. Of course all the things I have no control over like the plunging stock market, complaining clients and worry over the inability to get private health insurance due to the medications I am taking for an underactive thyroid and high blood pressure. I look like a risk on paper but I'm really very fit for my age. Insurance companies don't care that I exercise a couple times a day, a habit I have continued since I was in college. To them, on paper I just look like a fifty-four year old woman on the verge of a mental breakdown. When I'm not dreaming of the batting cage incident, I dream that I'm walking down the street in my J.Crew pea coat, all torn and tattered from the wear. I'm pushing a shopping cart down Main Street with all my belongings contained inside its wire basket. A poor, unfortunate soul who lost everything. People point and stare whispering, "Did you know that she used to be a successful stock broker?" Wake up! Wake up!

Equal Work for Equal Pay!

I want to believe we live in a world where people are accountable for their own actions. A world where people don't feel the need to *step on* others in order to get to the top. All we really want is to be treated fairly and considered equal partners in this world. What happened to all that work on the woman's movement, *woman's lib*? I'm afraid it has fallen on deaf ears. What does that mean and whose idea was it to think we could achieve it without a cost? Did it work, are we happy? My generation, the baby boomers wanted it all and expected to find happiness at the end of that rainbow in the form of a big pot of money and material things. I was thinking about this subject while walking today (where I do my best thinking). Maybe I have been looking at this all wrong. Why would I want to be paid like a man and treated like a man? Men can't multi-task. Most of the brokers in the offices in the past could barely get themselves to work in one piece. They often shined their shoes once they got in the office, many finished getting dressed walking around with their tie just hanging around their neck like a scarf, intending to tie it sometime. The manager of one of the firms ate cereal while walking from office to office dripping milk and slurping it like a kid. What planet were these men from anyway? I was one of the few brokers who made it in before the stock market opened in the morning. I walked in fully dressed, having eaten my breakfast at home, Nadia was fed, a sack lunch made and the thirty mile commute traveled. I had made it to the bus stop to meet the school bus on time often stopping first at the stationary store to pick up a required notebook or protractor necessary for class that day. It was just a typical morning in the life of Lisa Hitchcock.

Maybe life is just one big test while on this earth. Am I on the right track? Someone please tell me? I'm afraid I'm not pulling even a passing grade these days. These storms keep rolling in and I'm faced once again with the decision to admit defeat and retreat or ride it out. Right now, I'm choosing to wait and be patient.

In Pursuit of Life's Purpose

Maybe I want too many answers. Maybe it's enough to set our intentions and wait. We raise our children to be good citizens, accountable and independent and to make something of them-selves while they give back. My daughter has exceeded all my expectations in that regard. I'm so proud of her. Now I just need to figure out what I'm going to do with the rest of my life. Or not! There's that controlling part of me needing to know the future and forgetting to stay here in the *here and now*. I look at others my age, traveling and enjoying pre-retirement or retirement itself. I'm juggling a mortgage, bills left over from Nadia's month long study abroad in Florence, Italy last summer as my income continues to drop with this ailing stock market. My short term goals: to make sure I have money left for a nice bottle of pinot and add another foreign film to my *Netflix* favorites so I get it in time for the weekend. I sit at my favorite little table and chairs in my back yard and pretend I'm in Tuscany writing this book instead of Grass Valley. It would prove to be so much more inspirational.

Color Me Surprised!

I've always taken my role as an *old-school* stock broker seriously. For twenty five years I've tried to do the best for everyone I worked with. As a result many of my clients have become close friends over the years. I've attended weddings, funerals, Eagle Scout ceremonies, holiday parties and anniversary celebrations. I've shared in their proudest moments with their kids and grandkids and they have in turn, followed Nadia's life and her accomplishments. I've been more than just their advisor. But because I'm a woman broker, I've had to walk that fine line with clients that I shouldn't have been expected to. I'm talking about the ones who stepped over that line, the married ones who tried to make the relationship more than just broker client. It put me in a precarious position too many times to count. I didn't want to lose their business yet I wouldn't compromise my ethics and waiver on my moral standards. I resent that part. It wasn't enough to just do a good job and care about them as clients. I had to delicately keep *my guard* up without disturbing their fragile male ego.

I don't mean to stereotype here. There are men out there who have been victims of discrimination by women as well. It just isn't the norm. Either way it is unfortunate when it becomes a daily part of your work life and it costs you business and money. I can't believe this will not be made right by me someday. It every situation up until now, I have walked away instead of standing my ground and pointing figures. As a result, I have a hard time trusting men anymore. It has gotten in the way of relationships that maybe could have worked out but I wasn't willing to stick it out and see. Once the first little red flag goes up in my head it's *adios amigos!* I could devote an entire book to the topic of married men behaving badly but don't worry, I won't. I don't dare stir that caldron.

Like it or not, I'm now part of the *not so marketable group* in the workforce. The older women group that still needs to work but few companies want to hire. How did I get here after all these years of working and adding hard earned money into our social security system hoping there would be some left when I was ready to retire? I feel like women my age are throwaways, overlooked for younger women who aren't concerned with benefits becoming a part of their package. We are the generation that has sacrificed the most over our lifetime. I read recently that 87% of Americans believe that women have experienced age discrimination at some point in their lives. I don't see this percentage moving lower any time soon. I feel trapped in my career even though I know I have twenty or even thirty good working years left. I'd love to move in a new direction and uncover some of my many talents in another job that I enjoy. Unfortunately, if I leave, I give up the health insurance and it may not be available if I move elsewhere. Young people don't understand how valuable these benefits are in dollars. They are not yet in need of daily medications for thyroid, high blood pressure or sleep disorders, so it's a moot point for them. Women over fifty in the workforce should be rewarded at this time of their lives for improving the quality of life for our children and contributing to make this world a better place to live instead of being cast out to pasture like an old mare and told to keep our mouths closed and stop causing trouble.

I'm afraid that we, the women of the baby boomer generation, haven't come as far as we had hoped back in the 60s when it all seemed so exciting and new. Maybe some corporate offices are finally seeing the light, banning off color jokes and blocking disgusting e-mails and conducting annual meetings to discourage harassment in the work place. Too little too late, in my opinion. They are just being proactive to keep from getting sued. They must now follow protocol just in case some male co-worker decides to pat a women co-worker on the ass.

I experienced, first hand, harassment in many forms throughout my years in the brokerage business when I worked for the big wire house firms. Complaints to management fell on deaf ears and were swept under the rug. Often the issues involved management and they were simply reprimanded while the situation continued. I ultimately found it impossible to continue working under those conditions. Three years ago I finally joined a firm independent from the Wall Street, away from all the shenanigans and greed.

Words of Wisdom

I should have listened to you dad, your wise words advising me not to venture in this business. My grandmother's advice (the one who pictured me as Rose Queen) was a very forward thinker of her time. She said, "Become an interpreter, you'll always have a job". What a wonderful career choice that would have been now that our world is so internationally entwined. Maybe that's why I'm back in school taking Italian!

If I had followed the path of my parents, I would have most likely married one of my classmates. Then perhaps I would have found *happily ever after* sparing me from all these many learning experiences. Wanting more out of life has left me with *less* so many times. I seem to be facing yet another crossroad in my life which continues to stir up those same feeling on that merry-go-round in the park. It's my *merry-go-round life*. I put my needs on hold for so many years to be a parent. I now find myself alone in this peculiar place in my life, paralyzed by my circumstances and stuck in a life that goes round and round with no ultimate direction in sight. I'm afraid to get off the platform for fear of irreparable damage and regret.

I've spent this lifetime doing what I have believed is the right thing and tried to concentrate on being a good person. Along with work, I've put in years of volunteer work valuing the importance of giving back to my community. I try to be a good listener for my friends and I perform random acts of kindness as often as I can. I've tried to make contributions and not just make life all about me. Writing my thoughts over these last six months, while the stock market has plummeted, has proven to be necessary therapy. I guess that is why therapists recommend journaling. This is my journal, a very big journal. It has given me clarity and changed my focus. Before this process began I thought I was looking for a man to fill the void that Nadia left when she moved away. I wanted to be *rescued* more than *nurtured*, so I thought. The more I searched, the more disappointed I became. I almost settled many times and risked becoming the very person I liked the least, the victim!

I've been in love once and felt that joy of sharing life and its experiences with a soul mate. Maybe that was it. After all, some people never get to experience that in their lifetime. It wasn't forever but now every time I try to date, all others seem to fall short. Men and women are so different. Why can't men figure out how to use the air freshener in the bathroom and why don't they get it that we don't like huge speakers in the living room that rattle the walls when the bass is turned up too high? Who wants a whole refrigerator shelf taken up with beer? I don't want to start ironing men's shirts or share a bed with someone who snores. I love to mow my own lawn and I'm perfectly capable of handling power tools and a chain saw. I have installed dimmer switches on the lights throughout my houses and I know how to fix sprinklers. I have learned to maneuver a truck through a heard of cattle and used a shot gun for *beast* control. I know what I need at this point in my life, a four legged companion, not two. I think I'll get a dog.

Women are going to rule the world someday. The sooner that happens the better. They need to be at the helm running the country without all this bickering and bi-partisanship. We just voted in a new black President hoping for **change** but the arguing hasn't stopped. It seems like more of the same to me. I'm hoping that our kids and grandkids will wake up, want change, and make it happen. Save our planet from self destruction. Nadia is running around with her *heart and wings*, a reminder that her mom fought every step of the way for her. I hope she will take the lead and run with it.

I'm tired of the battle and the fight, but I'll always give my all to the task at hand. It is who I am. Through this process of writing these words which have turned into a book, I have felt a sense of calm come over me as if I am finally owning up to these events in my life. I am allowing them to remain in the past which has freed me up to start new. Don't get me wrong, I don't want to completely forget the past. It is who I am today. I just want to let go of the anger and remove all blame. I was constructing a resume in my mind the other day, fantasizing over having a job I could really enjoy. What would it say? *Fifty something female, innovative in times of crisis, able to perform most tasks with a roll of duck tape and a pair of tweezers, insightful, mind reader, good listener and wise beyond her years.*

Would you hire such a person? If you ever found yourself stuck in a fox hole with someone in the middle of nowhere, believe you me, you'd want me in there with you. However this is a different world now, technology is changing every day. Put me in a room with left brained tech heads and I'm afraid I would fall short. I can't even pretend to know the difference between a ram and megahertz. How do you spell that by the way? Gigabytes sound like a snack served in my kitchen made with soy and tofu.

I have a girl friend who just turned fifty. She was agitated and dreading it. Why do we panic so about that number? It's just a number like any other. It should be embraced for what it is. Society has labeled that number as an *over the hill* for us. Beauty and youth is worshiped and the farther we get from that, the harder it becomes. People often tell me I don't look a day over forty. Why do I say, "thank you"? It's a back handed compliment really. You look forty but you are really fifty-four. It is what it is.

Once Nadia left I was suddenly forced to take inventory of where I was in my life. I began to reflect on what I have become. Is this really where I wanted to be right now? I have been in *mom over-drive* for so many years just reacting to the tasks at hand, working, parenting, and providing a home for us both it is now difficult to change gears. I must say, I haven't really stopped parenting even though she's moved out. I guess we, as parents, never really stop. I'm paying her rent and school expenses and there is that outrageous Verizon monthly cell phone bill! We're supposed to be in some family in-network plan but the bill is still over $100 bucks a month! They claim family and friends are free as long as they are **in** network. I'm going to have to make a new rule. No friends or family members are allowed to call if they aren't Verizon subscribers. That's the first thing I'll have to ask her when she's excited about a new guy or friend at school. "Are they on a Verizon plan?" instead of asking, "do they have nice parents?" What have I been reduced to? It may sound harsh but something's got to give.

When I get a phone call from Nadia I can tell with the first words out of her mouth whether she's upset, elated, rejected or just chatty about something on her mind. I remember the time she called, "Mom, my car sounds like there is a Harley stuck to the back bumper, what should I do? Who should I call?" That problem turned out to be a stolen catalytic converter. Four wheel drive vehicles are targets for theft since they sit up higher off the ground. Due to the sky rocketing price of platinum, thieves steal these parts to make a quick $50.00. My client's ex-husband happened to be a mechanic in Huntington Beach and saved the day. I reached him on the telephone and he arranged for her to get the car fixed. Then there was the call, "Mom, I'm baby-sitting Hayley and Joey and we're in the cookie store. Joey ate a cookie before I could stop him and I have no cash! They won't take my debit card for a $3.00 cookie. What do I do mom?" Granted we are separated by many miles but that doesn't stop me from being the problem solver. I'm her **person**, the one who helps her get out of her crisis no matter how big or small. We never finish being moms until the day we die, devoting ourselves to protecting our young like a mother bear and her cub. Some people kick the kids out the door and the kids never look back. Not this mom, it's been worth every sacrifice. I remember back on those sleepless nights when she was sick with a fever, my feelings of helpless when she had to go to the hospital and get her tonsils out. The first time she drove her car alone to school and I dropped to my knees praying she'd get there in one piece. Then you suddenly look in the mirror years later and hardly recognize the person looking back at you. Instantly, middle age has set in and you didn't notice the process. Stop this speeding train please! I want to get off before another ten years has gone by with just the blink of an eye!

New Years Eve, a Time for Reflection

I start to put on my running shoes prompting my new dog, Angie to start her excited howling ritual. She knows we are going out for a walk. I put her in the back of the car and we drive to this beautiful trail in Nevada City where the road goes on forever and the only traffic you encounter are people with their dogs, and cyclists enjoying the great view of pine trees and running streams. I feel God nudging me, reminding me that my life is already complete, as it is right now. It is going to be a good new year. I need to concentrate on worrying less and working on finding the joy in each day for what it has to offer. Make less lists and more memories. Let Nadia be who she is going to be without trying to control her every move. Stop living my life through her accomplishments. Accept the fact that the stock market is going to have these gyrations and no one really expects me to be able to predict the future. Stop hating my job and make the best of it. At least I have a job and people rely on me to do the best job possible. This is only one season out of many to come.

While walking I reflect on what is most important to me. It is my family and dear friends. In times of uncertainty we reach for what is real, keeping our loved ones close. When Nadia came home for Christmas for seven short days I watched her step off that escalator at the airport, all grown up. How amazing to think that this extraordinary person turned out to be so lovely and seemingly unscathed by my own imperfections. I often tell her she inherited all the good genes from both her father and me. She is an awesome human being with a sweet spirit and compassion for all mankind. I couldn't be more proud. She didn't inherit my insecurities or my controlling nature. I am so relieved! She lived under my roof and influence for all those years and managed to turn out relatively normal. Thank you God!

I suddenly feel a load come off my shoulders as Angie and I continue our walk. She turns around to smile at me, as she often does, just to check on me at the other end of that leash. I recollect all the relationships that have been hurtful over the years and one by one I make a mental note to forgive these people who have behaved inappropriately. Many didn't know any better and I'm sure I was often too sensitive and ultimately too defensive. We often attract and manifest the very thing we dwell on and try to avoid. I was sick of married men pursuing me yet it kept happening. I manifested that very thing I didn't want. It is so clear to me now. That is why it is so important for us to keep our thoughts only on what we want to have happen and on the positives in life.

I've been accused of building walls around my heart. I've been called *rigid and closed* and accused of hiding behind my daughter to avoid a relationship where I might be forced to open up. I have been told I act unilaterally without an open mind to other views. It is all true by the way. I admit it. But who wouldn't have become somewhat calloused by it all if put in my shoes? I've put up my defenses and built walls to survive.

Who knows? Maybe this will be the year when a man comes into my life and allows me to be myself. A man who has the patience to take the time to earn my trust and allow me to feel comfortable enough to let my guard down. It could happen, but for now, I'm leaving my armor on and I will do battle only if there's no other solution while protecting my heart. Angie is filling the void and emptiness nicely. She is my walking partner and my protector and is my perfect companion. In the meantime, I hope this healing process helps me move toward some celebration. The ability to embrace my losses with as much joy as I acknowledge my victories and accomplishments. After all, that is the key to life. Enjoy the journey and the life God gave us. Take the ups with the downs and realize they are both of equal importance in life. We need the rough patches to appreciate the good times.

I'm going to choose to look at this, my life right now, as good enough for today. I'm relieved that the chaos of the past year is finally behind me. It's similar to a process I go through when I paint a picture. When I think it is finally finished, I hold it up in front of a mirror, getting a different perspective, as if a stranger is looking at it for the first time. If the reflection looks good, I sign it right then and there, with my name and the date. It is now complete. I'm going to do that with my life. Sign it and date it and move forward. No looking back. The rest of my life begins now. As I am writing these final words there is a song playing in the background on my *iTunes* by *Natasha Bedingfield* as she sings *"take me away to better days, a secret place, a pocketful of sunshine...I know I'll be all right, just take me away."*

Thank you for reading my story.

~Lisa

* * * * *

Nadia called me from college last week asking me for *Pike stories* for a paper she was about to write in her creative writing class. As you are about to read in her Pike piece, you will see that she has this wonderful gift of engaging her readers and luring them into her story with a refreshing writing style. We both laughed hysterically as we reminisced and came up with more stories of our time in Pike. I think it was a process she needed to go through to remember just how special that time was for us both. Two mountain women in the woods making a darn good life for ourselves with memories that would last a lifetime. Her classmates loved it and couldn't fathom these things really happened. They were sorry to have it end, left wanting more. So to wrap things up, here is **Pike** from Nadia's perspective for your enjoyment!

Pike

A Mother-Daughter Story
From a Daughter's Perspective

by

Nadia Hitchcock

Introduction

As a child, we all have mixed feelings about growing up. Desiring to fit in, while wearing the perfect pair of shoes, clean enough so it does not look as though your family is struggling yet dirty enough that you don't stand out *too* much. My shoes on the other hand, were always dirty because I grew up in the mountains where I could not wait to get outside and run about my twenty acres of precious land in the middle of nowhere so far away from school and friends. It was the age of fantasies and fairy tales which always ended with love and happiness. I would run about dancing and imagining I was a princess in a far away kingdom waiting upon my prince to rescue me. My mother would stop from her yard work and watch me race around the yard, playing till the sun began to set behind the mountains. Seeing my happiness shine around me seemed to please her. I was her reason for moving to Pike and I was the reason we moved away eight years later, in search of the next best thing.

A series of small serendipities is the only way I can sum up my childhood. Even through the many efforts my mom and I struggled through, each was beneficial in hindsight and formed our unique bond. More than a mother and daughter; held together by hope and love, we are and always will be, best friends.

Even at the age of twenty I still play, although I no longer believe in fairy tales, I do believe in reality though, which is far more powerful than the best fairy tale story. Each story created with the one you love is the best story ever written.

This is my story. It is not a fictitious tale. Only pure and true. There will be neither princes nor princesses. Neither dragons nor pirates. Although you will be entertained by bear stories, traffic jams due to cattle drives, Taco Tuesday's accompanied by drunk men with no teeth, shoot-offs in our front yard, fights with crazy animals and two women surviving in this tiny extraordinary town.

Pike

"How much you *throwin* down on the table, Jed?" the man said after taking a swig of his beer like it was his lifeline. "Oh I'll bet 100 beers those two blond prima donnas' won't last more than a month out here." Another man sucked in his cigar through his missing front tooth and competed from across the round table, "I'll take your hundred beers and bet you a hundred dollars they won't last more than a week!" Laughter swept over the room. "Do you got any 2s Joe?"
"Go fish!" Joe replied.

This is a typical conversation among the unemployed men of Pike. They could be found day or night huddled together at the famous bar located just out of town, properly called the *Brass Rail*. (The **B** and **r** light bulbs upon the shining sign were, coincidently, always burned out, leaving the brilliant new name ass rail.) Quite appropriately named if you ask me. Historically, Pike was an important part of the Gold Rush movement in the 1850s. Pike was nothing more than a farm house surrounded by miles of luscious red and green apple orchards. It was considered home to the miners of the *16-to-1 Gold Mine*. The miners were said to have piled on top of one another in a horse and buggy and make the twelve mile trek due north to Alleghany where they would spend long days underground searching for their fortune. Each evening at sundown they would head back to Pike singing in unison to the clang of the horse's shoes in trot. The *16-to-1 Mine* in Alleghany was still in operation while we lived up there, and to my knowledge was one of the only working gold mines left in California. Visiting that tiny town felt like a step back in time to the 1800s.

Pike, a tiny community that lived up to its short name. A town made up of a whopping 128 people and so small they did not even bother presenting it with its own zip code. Residents were forced to use the zip code from a nearby town of less distinction, North San Juan. Pike's population climbed to 130 when we purchased our home on *23 Wild Rose Meadow Lane*. Thank goodness for return address labels or it would have been quite tedious sending out Christmas cards and writing out a return address like this. We didn't receive much mail. Bills got routed to our P.O. Box in town. We called any mail that made it to our Pike mail box, *happy mail*. Not too many surprise guests paid visits to us either, considering it was tucked away, 30 miles from civilization. Miles and miles of winding roads that would cause any sensitive stomach to pull over. But once the belly became immune and your eyes were able to move their gaze from the dreaded brown bag to the climbing, one-lane road, lined with pine tree after pine tree welcoming your arrival, peace and serenity is found in this whistle-stop town. Refreshing and secretive, Pike had purposefully maintained itself, attracting all eyes, yet filtering its residents.

T.G.I.F had a whole different meaning in Pike. It meant horseshoes on the uneven lawns with beer in coolers and ultimately another reason to drink too much at the *ass Rail* complete with a return trip in the morning for the hair of the dog. Every Friday residents looked forward to the *Mountain Messenger*, the local Sierra County paper delivered to their mailboxes highlighting all the news from the week. Here you could read up on the latest information or events. It was Pike's version of E!—Entertainment News, a Sierra County gossip column. It was always packed with something fascinating that you would not want to miss. Headlines included *"Goldilocks and Bear"*?! One headline particularly memorable, starring the Jam Lady, a lady in her 70s who was famous for her mouthwatering jam which won awards at the annual *Alleghany Days Street* fair every year. True story, one morning she awoke, petrified to find a bear in her bed spooning next to her! Apparently the bear was as surprised and ran out when she screamed.

The police blotter was a town favorite in that paper with information on drunken arrests, cars wandering over the edge of the road, or my personal favorite, harvest time. In Alleghany guns would come out at harvest and break into a full blown shooting war between drunken men, resembling the shoot-offs of the western days. These juicy stories were great to read as a family while cuddling in front of the fire. If you didn't read it in the <u>Mountain Messenger</u>, not to worry because the guy who worked at the dump Saturday and Sunday would gladly fill you in and inform you of all the dirty details. One of the perks of the job!

At the end of our road lived our neighbors including three loud peacocks, two tire-biting dogs and one vicious cat. This house was set upon a hill with an arresting view of the mountains, peeking from the grouping of tall pine trees. But as you entered through their gate the beautiful view became obstructed by exposed junk cars, broken wood doors, scattered beer cans shot with a hole in the heart and a myriad of clutter half of which I was never able to identify. As neighbors we did our best to be friendly and approachable—although not comfortable enough to borrow an egg or two for baking, or maybe it was simply taking precaution of their eggs. The occasional exchange of wave as they passed by our house each day was enough bonding. It came as a surprise when they asked us to tend to their animals while they were going to be away on vacation. We consented without hesitation. "This is great!" my mom said to me, "We will be able to leave the house in better shape than when they left and with happy, fed animals." Being the clean freak she is she could hardly wait to do her part and tidy up their place. For sure they would come back impressed to see what capable, nice neighbors we were.

The morning after their departure we woke up ten minutes early in order to stop by their house before we journeyed down the long road for work and school beginning with that darn cat. Upon opening and stepping over the threshold, we pushed through the stuffy air and the aroma of a lovely mixture of cat feces and litter ushered us through the house. We were unable to grasp how the cat could have done so much damage in such a short amount of time. Surely the neighbors had cleaned the litter box and given the cat fresh water and food before they left...you would think! We began calling for the cat while choosing to follow our footsteps, instead of our noses to the back of the house. "Here Kitty Kitty Kitty!" we called sweetly, expecting to see a precious cat run towards our soothing voice in response. "Kitty Kitttttty", we emphasized, still searching for the lost creature. Nothing, nada, no sign of a cat. Just as we beginning to worry, I walked by the bed and FLASH! I was struck by the claws of the beast. Hissing, growling and howling came from beneath the bed. I screamed, taken by surprise. "What happened?" Mom hollered from the next room. "I found the cat" was my dry reply. "ggghhhhrrowww" the cat cursed at me from beneath its fortress in hell. My mom entered the room. "Where is he?" Just as she walked past the bed FLASH! Even swifter than before the blur hissed and attacked my mother's perfect ankles draped with newly torn tights. "Right there," I retorted, looking down in shock and frustration. Now out of self-defense we quickly began pouring food in the cat bowls, and cleaning up the exterior of the shit box, since this cat clearly did not believe in doing his business anywhere but the perimeter of his lavatory. I suppose he could have been attempting to conserve litter. The beast continued to wail wanting us to get out. We jumped to avoid his paws reach, as we left the room. The remaining days we came equipped in defensive gear—muck boots clear to my knees, prepared for a brawl. "Ha ha what are you going to do now kitty?!" I yelled. Not amused, all he gave me was a "hissss" in return. This was not his way of surrendering.

The dogs were another story. Cute dogs, right?! Yes, but they were lacking one necessary quality, common sense when it came to cars. My poor mother's leg, now bleeding as we locked the house and quickly fed the dogs. She was afraid there was no time to stop by the house and wash her battle wound but assured me she would purchase some new tights once we reached town. Leaving the hounds to devour their food, or so we thought, we began to drive off. They barked and started after us. Looking in her rear view mirror, my mother began to worry, "I hear them but I cannot see them!" She muttered something unpleasant under her breath and then ordered me to get out of the car and stand with them so she could start driving away without running one over. I do as she asks. She often forgot the fact that I was only 8 years old and with a tiny frame—and this request seemed nearly impossible. We were desperate and were going to be late for my bus if we didn't get out of there soon. I coaxed both dogs into a fenced area near the peacock yard, quickly shut the gate and ran! Swinging the car door open, practically while the car still moved, I hopped in. My mother's eyes shifted to the rear view mirror, like they do in horror films when the character feels the presence of a serial killer in the back seat. "How the h..." she began to say as I looked behind to see the dog running after us up the gravel road. She pushed the pedal down to the floor and sped up the road leaving a dirty cloud of rock and dust in our wake. Once we reached the main road we sped to town. Yeah! no sign of the dogs. Unfortunately, this was a routine that repeated itself for the next week. Each morning we shut the dogs behind the gate and made our getaway like a scene right out of a James Bond movie. We jumped in the truck and it became a race against paws. Until the worst happened. About a week into this ridiculous routine and completely fed up with the dog mess, we were driving away as usual, pedal to the metal, until our view in the rear mirror showed the dogs in hot pursuit and barking as if herding cattle. My mother's eyes once again fixed on the mirror, "Do you see them?!" she screamed. "Yes I do...wait no. Not anymore." "You can't see them? Or can you?" she asked again. "Well I see one" was my response "but I don't see...." suddenly we were interrupted by a heart stopping thump. My mother gasped. Her eyes filled with immediate tears. I sat in silence and couldn't help but look back. Yelping is all I heard. "It looks like we ran over her paw, mom." But we both knew it was not just her paw. Fumbling for her phone, my mother immediately called the fire chief, who conveniently lived down the street. It was a quick death, we were told. For the next few nights worry hovered over our home and our tired eyes could not sleep well. We decided to write an apologetic note of remorse. Once the neighbors returned home (a week later than expected) my mom felt she had to confront them about the situation. "Oh, it was bound to happen" was their insensitive response. The sweltering agony we had gone through and to see them react as though we had freed them of a burden. We were appalled.

Within a month they had a new dog. And wouldn't you know it, this one hunted cars like a predator hunts for its prey. It goes without saying, we were never again asked to watch their animals. Quite frankly, this was fine with us.

In Pike, there were no strip malls to shop at, pizza delivery was not possible, and the nearest gas station was ten miles south, there was not even a grocery store at which to pick up a late night necessity. There was a fire station though, volunteer. Pike was proud of this distinctive attribute. We used to ridicule by saying at least we do not have to worry if there is ever a fire. If the station had been as far as everything else, there'd be no point in attempting to save a thing. No hose would help by the time they'd get to us an hour later. Although we were safer than others, each summer we'd still cross our fingers every time we'd hear the news of yet another fire. The overpopulated plant life and dry heat caused much combustion during the summer. Luckily, the fire chief just so happened to live down the street from us. This was comforting, we thought.

One evening in the comfort of his home he received a surprising fire call. Flames were engulfing *his own* home! Racing outside to go to work, he was able to attack the blaze with a garden hose. Only damaging his front deck in the process. Dumfounded when he came to find out that the arsonist was his own wife! Irony is always so amusing. Talk about work interfering with your home life. Turns out the *unhappy* woman had been feeling neglected by her husband due to his busy work schedule and nights out with the boys. Needy as can be, she wanted to get his attention somehow.

Taco Tuesdays, two mouthwatering tacos, each shell sprinkled lightly with parmesan cheese and stuffed to the maximum with the goods and side of beans, salsa and chips, for a very small price. This was gourmet dining considering the location, let me tell ya. My stomach growled and ached each day on the ride home and I constantly begged for a snack to hold me over. During the long haul one evening, the sign advertising *Taco Tuesdays!*" caught my eye. "Mom! Let's stop! They are featuring Taco Tuesdays at *Peterson's Corner*". My mom glanced at the Harley bikes lined in front of the bar, which we considered the *half-way-point* to home. Strategically placed in the middle of nothing, was a very large sign that read *Beer and Ice* in big bold letters. Couldn't miss it which is why we had always made this the meeting place for the parents of my friends. We were doing them a favor by not making them endure the questionable drive through North San Juan. In looking back, by the looks of the people loitering there, I'm surprised the parents allowed their child to come visit me again.

My mom gave in and pulled the car over that first time. Excited, I jumped out of our pick-up truck and ran inside. I remember pulling on the heavy door and as I entered and inhaled a thick vapor of cigarette smoke. I crinkled my nose in disgust and looked back at my mother behind me, dressed so nicely in her work pant suit and heels. The sound of her heels clanking against the floor woke up the beast. The beast being men that is, who were all clearly not in a sober state giving us a toothless grin as we entered. A woman, who actually had some teeth yelled from the behind the bar and told us to take a seat anywhere. We walked around pool tables and sat at a booth, the head of a stuffed buck glared down from the wall, at our innocent faces. I begged my mom for quarters, and skipped over to the jukebox. I scanned through an array of country music, a collection of *Michael Jackson*, and too much *Enya* to know what to do with. I finally decide on *Man I feel like a Woman* by *Shania Twain* and a few others. Then my eyes light up —Now let me inform you, my mother and I have always been big *Eminem* fans— I see the words *Lose Yourself* and about lose myself with excitement. I skip back over to the table and plop down with a giggle. Shortly after a folk tune ends, I hear the familiar words blast through the speaker "I'm goin' out tonight, I'm feelin' alright, gonna let it all hang out..." My mom laughs in hysteria. I giggle and smile proudly at her reaction. The men sure stopped smiling fast. We received our taco feast which—hands down—still stands as the best taco Tuesday experience (buck head and all). As it quieted down the sound of a piano played through the speaker then was taken over by a strong beat followed by rapping. I began to rap along with each word, nodding my head to the beat and moving my hand back and forth enjoying my taco. My mother laughed so hard she had tears in her eyes. We overheard a man at the bar adamantly complaining about the music blasting through the speakers and before I could finish my rap, the jukebox was unplugged.

No Blockbuster Video in Pike, no liquor stores, no *Starbucks*, although there was a school. It was a very small, country school. The students, ranged from grades 4th-12th, gathered together in one classroom each day where they would learn together by helping one another. I'm sure it was lovely, but we decided I would go elsewhere for my education. In 2004 the graduating class was a whopping two people! The Valedictorian turned to me with pride and informed me of his noteworthy accomplishments. I held back my impertinent giggles (the only other student that graduated with him that year was mentally challenged). *As Valedictorian* he felt sure he could get a scholarship into an Ivy League school. Who was I to burst his bubble? I stroked his ego in return with congratulations and an abundant amount of head nods and wows. After all, the application to get into college didn't need to include the fact that he was simply salutatorian of two.

Cattle have their own personal rights in Sierra County. If you do not wish to have them on your deck, making dessert of your flower arrangements, or sculpting your front lawn, then put up a fence to keep them out. The pedestrian crossing signs beside the road are replaced with cow crossing signs in this region. Yes, a triangular yellow sign with the image of a cow pasted in the center does in fact exist. All summer the cows would roam the countryside heading north in attempt to get cooler. They would eat their way to the top by the end of the summer, taking their time. Every once in a while a fast car would race around the steep corners of the road and encounter the animal. This, of course, would make the headline of the *Mountain Messenger,*" *Car Killed by Cow!*" It was rumored that rear ending a cow could cause more damage than the impact of another vehicle. By the time fall rolled around the herders would mount their horses and retrieve their best dogs and begin from the top, gathering the cows and would slowly guide the cattle down the hill to a large pasture at the lowest part, in preparation for the cold winter. One Saturday morning my mom and I began the drive down the hill, from Pike, headed to town for a birthday party I was invited to. Along the way we ran into some traffic—a cattle drive hold-up. We worried about arriving to the party on time, but laughed hysterically at the unique situation; wondering if the explanation of being *stuck behind cattle* would be a believable excuse. While on the phone with the parents of my friend, the sound of cow bells, moooing and barking muffled our voice's yet defended our out-of-the-ballpark excuse. After a half an hour of creeping and crawling behind the cows, getting a quick lesson in herding for the day, dodging cow feces, we finally came to an area where we could pass. We waved out the window at the cows as we left them to their march, they mooooed and chewed their cud in reply.

Dope, grass, weed, hemp, Mary Jane, bud, hash, reefer, medicinal marijuana; many names for the same thing. It was the area's most valuable crop. Little green plants held high with prestige in this small, productive, green, secluded county. To most, growing marijuana was simply a way of supplementing their income. When we first moved into our home, there was a hidden trap door leading under the house with barely enough head room to stand, back straight. The side wall lined with at least fifteen lamps clamped onto the wooden posts and florescent lighting aimed at a long display shelf. A friendly neighbor down the road grew it for his sister, strictly for *medicinal purposes* of course. Each time we saw him, he had a big grin pasted on his face and never went any-where without his five German Shepherds respecting his every command. A gate was the first thing to go up at the entrance of his property, naming his territory, *Sheperd Sanctuary* (we assumed the misspelled word was intentional) when he began to build his log *mansion*. He was a reclusive character but nice. He introduced himself when he started building his log home himself, his long dark hair pulled back in a pony tail, his jeans barely clinging on to his long, skinny frame. The hair above his lip tickled him as he smiled, always conversing in a louder-than-necessary, voice. He was so proud of his tractor and was very helpful around our prop-erty and he was a *host with the most* once his home was completed. In fact Wednesday evening turned into a weekly men's poker night at his log cabin down the gravel road. Who knows what exactly was going down there, but it didn't take him long to fit in. He was really proud of his *crop* and shared it with selected vis-itors. All too frequently the cops would drive down our gravel road and hike a half a mile to his front door to keep tabs on his garden.

Having pets in Pike did not seem limited to our two cats and one dog. It was a jungle out there. Lions? no, tigers? not quite, but bears? most definitely. Often we would find their feces in big piles throughout our 20 acres of backyard or footprints in the snow. Luckily we had never encountered a bear face to face while roaming the property. My mother would warn me, "Always run down hill! They can't run well down hills." She would say this as we would make the haul up the hill to our house, clearly uphill. "So in other words" I said, if I am down here and I run into a bear, I'm screwed because the only way home is up! Comforting thought!"

One evening I remember vividly. I was relaxing downstairs in our house watching television. I heard a loud bang from above me which sounding like our gate slamming shut. I did not think any-thing of it considering my mother was always out and about doing projects that consisted of many strange noises. I heard the gate rattle a second time. Since it was getting late, I decided to see what she was up to. I rolled my eyes as I pulled myself out of my comfortable position and walked up the stairs. "Mom what are you doing?!" I said, somewhat annoyed. She responded from her room: "I'm getting ready for bed!" What caught my eye shocked me as I reached the top step. Standing outside our French doors on our deck was a large brown bear. "Mommmm! There's a bear on our deck." I spoke in a surprisingly calm tone. She ran out of her room. "What?!" As she ran down the hall the bear ran off our deck, its nails gripping the wood as it hurried away. Like curious children, my mom and I ran to the kitchen window to spot its location. There standing below the window was the big brown bear searching for food. My mom is gone again now, rummaging through her closet. She returned with a 410 shot gun and ammunition in her other hand. She began to attempt to load the gun but nerves had her fingers shaking. "Do you want me to load the...." "No!" she interrupted, "I can do it." After a moment the gun was loaded. Mom stopped shaking - for the most part. We both assume position on the front line—our deck. Our target has now moved to the grass lawn, looking for anything to munch on. "Now of course we do not want to shoot him" my mom explained to me. "Yea, cause then we would have a dead bear on our lawn. That may be hard to hide." BANG! The gun sounded. The bullet shot just by the bear's foot causing him to move as fast as the bullet, heading into the opposite direction of our home. The sound throbbed my earlobes and caused a slight ringing for about a minute. I looked at my mother's face - pure shock. "I didn't know bears could run so fast," I exclaimed. "Me neither." My mom said, still in shock. In my head I heard the gunshot repeat and saw the bear race off. My mother grabbed my hand and put it over her racing heart. Thump, thump. Thump, thump. "Good job mom! You've gotta be the only mom who knows how to use a shot gun - and use it well!" She laughed and guided me back into the house.

"When I take risks and put my all into a relationship with a guy and he becomes *the guy* I'm looking for then I find myself no longer desiring him. It's as though all the work wore me out so much that I am ready to recycle and just be free. It's funny how life works. A friend of mine explained this concept to me. Maybe that is why my mom finally decided to move away from Pike. The desire was gone.

The news of our house back on the market spread like a wild fire. The fire dispersed just as quickly as the news of our arrival had, eight years prior. Our clutter-filled, simple home was transformed into an elegant retreat during those years. My mother had put so much hard work into this *money pit* and as much as she loved the place, it was going to make her crazy like everyone else in the little town. You cannot live there and see the larger picture. Life was so small to these residents but they had chosen the lifestyle and seemed satisfied. They were right to think of us as different, but they were wrong to assume we could not successfully survive. After all, we were the ones they began to ask favors of. They began free loading, the two southern-California-born girls whom they assumed were not good for anything except standing still and looking nice. They would walk into our shed and help themselves to extra gas and oil when they ran dry; they drove down our driveway in search of firewood when they did not properly prepare for extra cold winters; they casually asked us to get items in town since we were already making the long haul each day for work and school; and thought it was just fine to drive down our property when we were not present to try to remove the boat that they insisted was theirs. My mother and I became the convenience store of Pike. The *Shell Answer Man*. What they did not know is that mom had a rifle that she was not afraid to use.

I walk out the front door, the screen slams behind me. On my back is a backpack full of crackers, raisins, box juices, books, a blanket, my favorite stuffed animal, underwear and a toothbrush. In my right hand I carry my oversized cat squished into her carrier, howling to get out. In my left hand is a leash attached to my sweet Labrador retriever, with her tongue hanging out of the side of her jowls. I walk with my baggage up our gravel driveway, dressed in my blue jeans and my favorite red Hurley sweatshirt with holes in the sleeves and a baseball cap pulled tightly over my head. I glance at my mother out of the corner of my eye who is diligently feeding the fire blazing from pit with broken wooden chairs, pieces of ply wood, and other various junk still being found on the "back 40" (the name we proudly gave to our property of 20 acres). She turns her attention in my direction as I pass. "Sweetie! What are you doing?" My mother asks, concerned. "I'm running away." I reply without any eye contact. Really?!...uhhh...Where will you go?" "North San Juan." I reply with confidence. Trying to think back on all those parenting books, yet no chapter on *what to do when your 7 year old try's to run away*, the obvious panic she was feeling didn't show on my mother's face. "Ok..." she said.

I continue my walk up the driveway and soon stop. My mother stacks more debris on the fire and slyly peeks at me out of the corner of her eye. I stare at nothing but pine trees and an open sky leading my way. I decide to rest my arm because my cat is really heavy and I need to rest it before the long journey. As I sit I ponder. Here I am in this new home, out in the middle of nowhere—knows nobody, and nothing. It seemed fun and different when I saw it for the first time but now I'm ready to go back. Go back to what is comfortable.

First time I was introduced to our big home I was overwhelmed. I had never lived in a place with so much land and so much...nothing! Exceptional nothing, though. Green grass, colorful wild flowers sprouting all about, blackberry bushes taking over, fire wood stacked tall, and a breathtaking view of nothing but pine trees and mountains. So much more spacious than the tiny house we had been renting in town. The best part though was the fact that I could finally get the dog that I had always wanted! The long blue roof spread on the top of our new home and I stared in amazement. I had never seen a roof this color before, this was another naive reason why I liked this home. The main reason I was so willing to move here with my mother, yet again, was because this house was *it* for her. This house was going to save her. Save us, that is. I could tell. I was ecstatic that first night in Pike! I put things in their places in my new big room and fell asleep upon my large double mattress with new crisp pink sheets. My mother dragged her mattress onto the deck and fell asleep gazing at the clear constellations above. Surprisingly, I had no urge to get up and sleep next to her that night. This was our sanctuary, our very own.

As I began to grow, I fell in love with the place. I would play outside until it got dark while my mother worked, stacking wood, laying concrete, applying stakes, putting up fences, taking down fences, planting flowers, moving boulders; constantly the sounds of drills and hammers would echo our names through the neighborhood. Often I would yell from the deck to my mother, working hard in her sleeveless shirt, her shoulders standing strong— "What time is dinner?!" I became a professional at making top raman and e-z mac and cheese. Don't get me wrong, my mother is a phenomenal cook; no one can cook a steak like her on an open bon fire, hands down. Living in Pike, there was always so much work to be accomplished and never enough daylight to do it all.

One Christmas I longed to have my own video camera and was overwhelmed with joy when Santa found Pike and delivered my very own video camera for me that year. My friends would come over for the weekend to stay, since it was not a short drive, and I'd set that camera up on the tri-pod and we'd dress up and make feature films. I soon taught myself to edit them into short features with music and credits. On my 16th birthday I had a blast riding in a hummer limo home with my girlfriends for an overnight and making a Christina Aguilera music video.

While entering into my teen years my priorities changed. I became less carefree and more...well, like a teenager. I began to hide my interests in film and began to despise Pike. Boys became interested in me and I would stay up late at night to speak online with them, watching the hours speed by. Although many boys considered dating me, we decided the one's who made the hour long drive to see me or pick me up were the only ones really worth the time. Especially when cash for gas was not even asked for. These were the days I began to imagine of living in town. I longed to sleep in not having to wake up at 4:30 in morning for school. I hated having to do my makeup in the car during the 45 min drive down the hill to town and having to go to my mom's office by 6:30, when the stock market opened. I then had to catch my school bus at 7:15 for school. We found ourselves doing a lot of driving. And when I began to drive it was a whole other story. Learning how to drive on sinuous cliff roads, maybe passing 5 cars (if you're lucky) the entire 40 minutes to town. It was challenging, dodging deer, many stupid squirrels and cows, all while trying to tune out your mother's frightened screams around every corner. Let's just say, I did not pass my first three driving tests in town and had to go through the whole process twice —although I always aced the written test. I finally took the drivers test with my father in Southern California and I did just fine in his Prius and normal streets.

Back to my *running away* story: My mother hollered at me from her large bon fire reaching five feet from the ground, "I'm going to put some steaks on the grill soon, should I put one on for you?" I sat and stared off into the open wilderness, in deep thought, wondering what will become of my life in this strange, big, quiet place, but as I think I can't predict what will happen. This is comforting to me, because even though I have no idea of what will come of this place I know I will always have her. I stared back, dog still controlled by leash and my cats face pushed up against the cage, trying to escape. My mom stared at me, smiling, with the question still on her face—I smiled and stood. Opening the carrier and I released my obese kitty and bent over and un-hooked the leash upon my dog's collar. She looks back at me as if to get my approval, I look over and say "I'm coming!" She continued to stoke the fire. I came over to her and responded, "Yes, I'm starving...can we make s'mores after?" My mother smiles. I glanced down to see two steaks already cooking on the grill.

Some people asked my mom why she left our beautiful home in Pike. "I moved up there to slow down and smell the roses and yet I found that I actually brought the rat race up there with me. I did not slow down as much as I had hoped. I actually created busyness up there as much as in town except for the lovely evenings spent on the porch swing and listening to the frogs sing. But grooming 20 acres was too much to take on. It became a never ending project. I felt like Sarah Winchester in a house never to be complete and that would work me to death." Others completely understood and didn't question our decision. We never again would visit that tiny town tucked out in the middle of nowhere, not because we detested the place - it was simply a life altering, grounding, time of transformation and building of character for both of us. There came a time when we were ready to begin our next chapter in a lovely Victorian on West Main, walking distance to Downtown Grass Valley.

The population returned to 128 people as we drove away from that green sign welcoming newcomers to Pike. With our frustrated cat howling from the back seat, we turned the music up to block the sound and thoughts. In the reflection of the window I watched the tears fill my mother's eyes. I let her cry in silence. I moved my attention to the trees, they gestured their goodbye in a blur while we sped past. We passed the *ass Rail* and heard a man holler our way. Staring out the window I yelled in the direction of the guys playing horse shoes, "Well guys, here goes the last bit of class left in Pike." I looked at mom and together we broke out in laughs of relief.

The first thing we did that first night in our new home in town was order pizza to be *delivered*. The first delivery pizza we had enjoyed in over 8 years. It tasted so good for so many reasons.

Now, living here in southern California, I look back on those years spent in that tiny town where I could run as far as my legs would take me. I am thankful for the lifestyle I grew up in and believe it molded me into the young woman I am today. Through my divergent upbringing I learned to become comfortable in what ever situation I find myself in even if it means stepping out of my comfort zone. Living in Pike taught me to make something out of nothing and how to get by, with very little.

How many girls can say they picked out their own Christmas trees each year by the road side, shaking the snow off the top first to see if the tree was worthy of our living room? Then cutting it down by themselves with a hack saw as the *Chipmunks Christmas song* blasted from the car stereo. It was a priceless tradition. Another tradition I'll never forget was the kindness of a Pike resident who decorated each mailbox in town always on the first day of December with multi-colored garland and Christmas balls. These decorations weathered all the rain, wind and snow throughout the month. Best part was she wore a Santa hat while delivering holiday cheer. So much joy was brought to each resident of that little town by this touching act of kindness. Each Christmas I think of her and turn my focus on the little things that make the season special and most of all the company of one another, family and friends.

I can't help but compare those times to now. Where I live today, material items are priorities and considered key to happiness. I grew up with people who did not have much. But the residents of Pike looked at life differently and through their eyes appreciated the beauty surrounding their life and the simple things which brought them pleasure. Even with all they lacked, they liked their life and seemed just as happy...maybe even happier.